AF560649

Reform in the Arab World

External Influences and Regional Debates

Talmiz Ahmad

India Research Press
New Delhi

India Research Press
B-4/22, Safdarjung Enclave, New Delhi – 110 029.
Ph.: 24694610; Fax: 24618637
e-mail : contact@indiaresearchpress.com; bahrisons@vsnl.com
www.indiaresearchpress.com

2005

ISBN : 81-87943-78-5

Cataloguing in Publication Data
Includes bibliographical references and index.
1. Middle East 2. Reforms 3. Arab
I. Title II. Author

Printed in India at Focus Impressions, New Delhi – 110 003.

It is refreshing that, for the first time in more than half a century, the political discourse in the world of Islam is increasingly dominated by the democratic lexicon.

-Amir Taheri, *Arab News*, April 21, 2004

Lest anyone misconstrue, let me affirm here, with as strong a conviction as I can make, that the leadership in Saudi Arabia remain steadfast in their effort to push their programme for reform. For us reform is an absolute requisite for the advancement of the country and its people regardless where the opposition is coming from or from where the external pressure is being applied.

-Saud Al-Faisal, Saudi Foreign Minister, April 27, 2004

For as long as whole regions of the world simmer in resentment and tyranny – prone to ideologies that feed hatred and excuse murder – violence will gather, and multiply in destructive power, and cross the most defended borders, and raise a mortal threat. There is only one force of history that can break the reign of hatred and resentment, and expose the pretensions of tyrants, and reward the hopes of the decent and tolerant, and that is the force of human freedom…So it is the policy of the United States to seek and support the growth of democratic movements and institutions in every nation and culture, with the ultimate goal of ending tyranny in our world.

- President Bush's Inaugural Address, January 20, 2005

To promote peace and stability in the broader Middle East, the United States will work with our friends in the region to fight the common threat of terror, while we encourage a higher standard of freedom. Hopeful reform is already taking hold in an arc from Morocco to Jordan to Bahrain. The government of Saudi Arabia can demonstrate its leadership in the region by expanding the role of its people in determining their future. And the great and proud nation of Egypt, which showed the way towards peace in the Middle East, can now show the way towards democracy in the Middle East.

- President Bush's State of the Union Address, February 2, 2005

The Bush administration must accept that it is too unpopular to issue a US-led greater Middle East initiative. American calls for region-wide reform and democracy are viewed as hypocritical and tailored to creating regimes friendly to the US and Israel.

Such an initiative will do more to undermine local reformers and label them as American tools than to push reform forward.

- Anthony Cordesman, *LA Times*, May 26, 2004

The story is told that one of the Caliph Omar's governors sent him a message asking for his permission to resort to repression in his district, saying: 'There are people here that nothing but the sword and the whip can set aright'. Omar, God rest his soul, responded: 'You lie; nothing but justice will set them aright. Spread justice amongst them.'

Preface

This monograph provides a glimpse of the contemporary reform ferment across the Arab world even as it describes attempts of Western countries led by the USA to influence the content, direction and pace of these aspirations. Given the rapidly evolving situation in the region, certain events mentioned in it may be overtaken by new developments. However, I believe that these will not affect the principal arguments presented here or the overview and prognosis attempted at the end.

This book is the result of my personal interaction with Arab lands and their peoples over 30 years, which has enabled me to obtain some understanding of their predicament as they cope with the numerous crises, internal and external, that all-too-frequently overwhelm them and leave in their wake a sense of despair and helplessness in not being able to control their destiny and shape their own future.

The presentation here reflects my personal understanding of the region and does not necessarily represent the views of the Ministry of External Affairs or of the Government of India, which I have had the privilege of serving both at home and abroad since 1974. Obviously, over the years, I have benefited greatly from the insights and advice of my colleagues in the Foreign Service, who have patiently guided my footsteps across the Arabian Peninsula and North Africa.

Above all, my encounter with the Arab world has been enriched by the support I have received from my wife, Sunita Mainee, who has been my partner in reaching out to and befriending the people we met in our postings and interacting with them with the sympathy and understanding that comes from the consciousness of one's own limitations and frailties. Hence, I dedicate this work to her as a tribute to her role in our diplomatic and personal engagement with the men and women of the Arab world.

New Delhi
March 2005

Talmiz Ahmad

Contents

Introduction

The Cold War was a relatively simple period: alliances were firm, strategic interests of partners were similar, and commitments were enduring. Through the Cold War, Saudi Arabia was the strategic ally of the United States, the two unlikely partners having to overcome obvious diversities on the basis of common interests: the United States provided security to the Kingdom, both against internal disorder and external threats, and, in turn, Saudi Arabia ensured stable oil supplies, and supported US interests in the region, in Iran, then in Afghanistan, and later in Iraq.

The two partners, with Pakistan, unitedly confronted the Soviet Union in Afghanistan. In so doing, they converted the Afghan national struggle into a global *jihad*. Thousands of Muslims rushed to Pakistan and Afghanistan in response to the call of their faith. Besides Pakistan, the bulk of these *jihadis* came from the Arab world; these Arab-Afghans fought side by side with the Afghan *mujahedeen* to liberate Afghanistan from Communist domination.

The certainties of the Cold War collapsed with the fall of the Berlin Wall. The Arab countries, in face of these cataclysmic changes in the world order, recognised the need for creative ideas to safeguard what was enduring in the earlier engagements even as they attempted to set up new arrangements to cope with the fresh challenges that now confronted them.

However, the invasion of Kuwait by Iraq ensured that the Arab world would not be able to examine the implications of this emerging new order in an environment of leisurely contemplation. The occupation of Kuwait unleashed a sense of crisis in the region as the Arabs saw the mobilisation of foreign armed forces within their borders to evict the aggressor. The leaders of the region were convinced that, for them, the emerging new order would not have benign implications, and that the challenges before them would not end with the eviction of Saddam's forces from Kuwait; they recognised that new regional realities would emerge which would severely test their political capabilities. They knew that the United States, even as it confronted Saddam's Iraq, would, after the Gulf War, maintain a long-term armed presence in the region, and would emerge as the single most significant role-player in the politics and strategic equations in the area. Their apprehensions came alive in the sanctions regime against Iraq, the UN-led inspections, the no-fly zones, and, above all, in the sustained US military presence in the region, all of which created an atmosphere of instability and uncertainty in the Arab world.

During the same period, the consequences of the *mujahedeen* struggle in Afghanistan also came to fruition: basking in their victory in the *jihad* against the atheist Communist, the Arab *jihadis* refused to melt away into the mundane commercial and consumerist milieu of their home countries. These *jihadis* had been imbued with the glory and perfection of Islam in the *madrasas* at the Pakistan-Afghanistan border; they had been provided fairly advanced training in combat and subversion, and had personally witnessed the success of their zeal and faith against a superpower. They could not, after this, tolerate the political order in their home countries characterised, in their view, by corruption, venality and repression, and sustained by alliances with non-Islamic Western countries. Nurtured in violence, they resorted to violence in defence of their faith against their enemies.

The sufferings of the Iraqi people during the 1990s as a result of the sanctions – inspections regime, the collapse of the Middle East peace process accompanied by increasing violence against the Palestinians, and, above all, the continued presence of foreign forces on Saudi and Arab soil, all of these came together to nourish Islamic extremism, which, at the end of the 20th century, challenged the political status quo in the Arab world.

The response of the Arab regimes to this political challenge posed by the US armed presence in the region and the anger of the *jihadis* was not particularly impressive. Instead of recognising that the new order posed new and unprecedented challenges, most regimes went back to their time-honoured practice of responding to these new realities tactically through a combination of coercion and co-option, without addressing or even recognising the need to confront the very obvious political, economic and social malaise that had, over the years, become the central characteristic of their polities.

During this period, there was certainly talk of reform: speeches were made, committees were set up, reports were prepared, but nothing really changed. The leaders believed that their irksome problems would in due course just disappear, as earlier problems had done, in face of the strong hand of the regime, coupled with promise of substantial financial reward for those who gave up dissent and came on board.

And, then, 9/11 happened. The Afghan *jihad* had now come a full circle and was devouring its creators. There had been warnings earlier that, in respect of these *jihadis*, policies of coercion and co-option were not actually working. There had been clear indications that these zealots were mobilising themselves in Sudan, in Yemen and, above all, in the territories controlled by the Taliban in Afghanistan, and that they were looking for fresh targets, as dramatically exemplified by the first attack on the World Trade Centre in February 1993; the attacks on Saudi and American targets in Riyadh and Dammam in 1995 and 1996; the attacks on the US Embassies in East Africa in 1998; and, in October 2000, the attack on the US naval ship, *USS Cole*, off Aden. Well before 9/11, Al-Qaeda had become a full-blown monster with its tentacles spread across the world.

September 11 provided a vision and a strategy to a US Presidency that until then had been groping for fresh ideas and a relevant foreign policy. The "global war on terror" now became an article of faith for the United States. Even as the US Administration unleashed its armed might against Afghanistan and Iraq and gave a free hand to Sharon's Israel to crush Palestinian resistance as part of the war on terror, the US Government, media and think-tanks turned their attention to Islam, the Arab world and Saudi Arabia, and held them responsible for the catastrophe unleashed upon the Americans.

Reform – of religion, of politics and economics, of education, and of cultural and religious life – this became a new buzz-word. The enthusiasm of the reform advocates was significantly buttressed by the contributions of neo-conservatives (neocons) who were dominant in the Bush Administration, and who saw in Middle East reform an opportunity to re-work the region so as to serve Israel's security interests and America's long-term political and economic agenda.

The Arab regimes saw a disintegration of the deep and abiding relationship they had had with America and its replacement with hostility and abuse. Every attempt they made to present their point of view and recover their traditional ties was systematically checkmated by the neocons and their allies in the Administration.

This new focus on reform, whatever the motivation of its protagonists, had the effect of igniting a reform-related debate across the Arab world. Academics, journalists, businessmen and political figures, and, frequently, government leaders, all of them participated in this resounding cacophony for reform, discussing issues of political, economic, social, religious and cultural change with unprecedented freedom; they frequently differed from each other in detail, and even principle, but were unanimous in conveying to their rulers that the status quo was no longer acceptable. The Americans and their Western allies attempted to contribute to this discussion and even tried to push it in directions that would suit their interests, but such interventions were generally unsuccessful owing to the conviction that real and enduring reform would have to emerge from within the Arab polities and would have to be a result of the Arab people's own efforts.

The discussion about reform is still in full flow, yielding in its wake some satisfaction that debates are underway in a relatively free atmosphere that will decide the destiny of the defeated and demoralised Arab person and, perhaps, hopefully, take him to a better future; there is also disappointment that so little has actually changed over three years after September 11, even as the political environment in the region continues to deteriorate.

This monograph provides an account of this extraordinary intellectual ferment in the Arab world and the attempts of governments, Arab and foreign, to cope politically and intellectually with these new challenges.

I. Background to the "Reform" Initiative

Within a few weeks of the September 11 events, US political leaders, academics and journalists began a scathing criticism of Saudi Arabia and Egypt, and of the Middle East in general, on account of the proven involvement of Arab nationals in the WTC/Pentagon attacks and the identification of the Taliban and Osama bin Laden as the source of this terror. Criticism in the US media revolved around two major premises:

(i) that the Middle East region was the source of terrorism against the United States; and

(ii) that it was a reluctant partner in the coalition against international terror led by the United States.

The view accepted by the US administration, and widely held in the US media and public opinion, was that autocracy and repression in the Middle East had meant denial of democracy and human rights to the vast populace, accompanied by economic stagnation and denial of employment opportunities and opportunities for creative self-expression and dignity. Since "Islam" was the only available institution to express anger and dissent, a number of young Arabs had been seduced by its blandishments, especially by the extreme groups that preached hatred of the West, particularly the USA, as the religious enemy and the upholder of the despised political authority. In terms of this analysis, the USA had been wrong to tolerate the repressive regimes in the Middle East as bastions of stability and allies in support of its interests, since these apparently "stable" polities had nurtured the most virulent of America's enemies – extremist Islam.

The US critique of "Islam" in the Middle East focused specifically on Saudi Arabia, given that at least 15 of the 9/11 hijackers were Saudi nationals; it consisted of the following points:

(i) Saudi Arabia espoused a fundamentalist and extreme form of Islam called Wahhabism which breeds holy warriors;

(ii) the Saudi education system nurtured hatred for Americans, Westerners, foreigners and all non-Muslims;

(iii) in order to boost its Islamic credentials and gain legitimacy, the Saudi royal family had, over the years, propagated the Wahhabi mindset and funded Al Qaeda/OBL/Taliban/other Islamic extremist groups in different parts of the world; and,

(iv) the Saudi authoritarian order and the corruption of the royal family had aroused deep-seated resentment in the Saudi populace which had no means of expressing itself except through rage against foreigners, particularly the USA; this populace has been brainwashed to hate the West, to see Islam under threat from the West, and to regard bin Laden and other terrorists as folk-heroes.

Flowing from this analysis, the course of action advocated for the Middle East was simple and sweeping — drastic political change in the region in favour of freedom, democracy and human rights. The *Washington Post*'s editorial of the time was typical: Starting with the major premise that the US knows that "its backing of the corrupt and authoritarian Saudi regime damages its image throughout the Middle East and makes it a target of terrorism," the paper argued that change in the Middle East must commence with the recognition that Saudi Arabia's domestic political order is a vital US interest, and that its autocratic system "is itself one of the root causes of Islamic extremism." The paper believed it was no longer reasonable to accept the "Saudi view that political change is unnecessary or excessively risky." It said: "Expanding personal and political liberty is necessary for stability in rapidly modernising societies, and is the best way to head off Islamic extremism."[1]

This view was echoed by the reputed US-based scholar of Arab origin, Fawaz Gerges, who noted that the Kingdom's strategy of "using religion as a legitimising device (is) potentially self-destructive and has led to the empowerment of the bin Laden phenomenon." As a solution, Gerges recommended "a clean break with past policies, in which the Saudis gradually open up their closed system and integrate rising social classes into the political field."[2]

This critique of the Saudi order and the rest of the Middle East was articulated most cogently and forcefully by the rightwing neo-conservatives (neocons) who exercised enormous influence over the Bush White House, particularly after 9/11. As a result of their efforts, in September 2002, one year after the 9/11 events, the Bush Administration promulgated its "National Security Strategy,"[3] enunciating a vision and a mission which, in true American tradition, came to be referred to as the "Bush doctrine". The doctrine was based on the conviction that :

> America is now threatened less by conquering states than we are by failing ones. We are menaced less by fleets and armies than by catastrophic technologies in the hands of the embittered few.

The doctrine provided a comprehensive exposition of the Administration's foreign policy strategy, dealing with US interests and objectives from defence to international economic policies and even environmental issues. It articulated a robust unilateral interventionist approach to reorder the global strategic environment in the long-term US interest. Priority attention in this regard would be paid to the Middle East.

Bush had already articulated his position in favour of reform in the Islamic world in his "State of the Union" Address, in January 2002, when he had said :

> America will lead by defending liberty and justice because they are right and true and unchanging for all people everywhere.... America will always stand firm for the non-negotiable demands of human dignity; the rule of law; limits on the power of the state; respect for women; private property; free speech; equal justice; and religious tolerance. *America will take the side of brave men and women who advocate these values around the world, including the Islamic world,*

> because we have a greater objective than eliminating threats and containing resentment. We seek a just and peaceful world beyond the war on terror. (Emphasis added.)[4]

Bush followed this general articulation with some specific remarks, on September 12, 2002, at the UN:

> The people of Iraq can shake off their captivity. They can one day join a democratic Afghanistan and a democratic Palestine, inspiring reforms throughout the Muslim world.[5]

The central feature of Bush's Middle East vision is "the determination to use America's unprecedented power to reshape the Middle East, supporting America's friends in the region, opposing its enemies and seeking to promote democracy and freedom."[6] This vision is based on two considered beliefs. First, that the status quo in West Asia is no longer acceptable. While for several decades America had substantial ties with repressive regimes in the Arab world, this arrangement is no longer tenable, primarily because, as 9/11 had shown, it had become a problem for America itself. The practice of the US's principal allies, the regimes of Saudi Arabia and Egypt, to maintain themselves in power by using "Islam" and tolerating/encouraging anti-American and anti-Israel positions in their population had, in the Administration's view, culminated in the attacks of 9/11, and today threatens US and Western security.

Secondly, in the long run, peace and stability and an end to anti-Westernism will not be possible until the region's regimes become more democratic. Philip

Gordon has noted that many of the big thinkers behind the Bush Administration's approach are imbued with "a neo-Wilsonian sense of idealism" that rejects European realism and cynicism about the possibility to spread freedom and democracy in the Arab world.[7] While the Bush officials accept that such a task would be difficult and time-consuming, they are convinced that the process should be begun and pursued through "muscular diplomacy, containment and, where necessary, use of force."[8]

Regime change in Iraq is the first step in this process. Iraq was expected to emerge as a model Arab country that is free, democratic and prosperous. The success of this model, as also the reduced US dependence on Saudi oil, would enable the Americans to vigorously pursue issues such as human rights, anti-Americanism and corruption. Over time, the people of the Arab world would come to see that freedom, liberal democracy and capitalism were the best principles on which to organise their society.

Rightwing writers applauded the approach: the journalist, Michael Kelly, wrote that a democratic Iraq and Palestine "will revolutionise the power dynamic in the Middle East....A majority of Arabs will come to see America as the essential ally."[9] The neocon intellectual, Joshua Muravchik, said: "Change towards democratic regimes in Tehran and Baghdad would unleash a tsunami across the Islamic world."[10] Another neocon intellectual, Michael Leeden, called upon the United States to launch:

a vast democratic revolution to liberate all the peoples of the Middle East... It is impossible to imagine that the Iranian people would tolerate tyranny in their own country once freedom had come to Iraq. Syria would follow in short order.[11]

The Arab Human Development Reports

The Bush Administration's agenda for democratic reform in the Middle East received support from an unexpected quarter : the publication of the *Arab Human Development Report* (AHDR) in July 2002.[12] This report was prepared by the UNDP and the Arab Fund for Economic and Social Development and written by a number of Arab intellectuals and members of NGOs, headed by the Egyptian intellectual, Nader Fergany.

The ADHR-2002 presented a devastatingly negative picture of the socio-economic situation in the Arab world compared with other regions. It spoke of three deficits in the Arab world relating to freedom, empowerment of women, and knowledge. The report, *inter alia,* noted :

(i) Over the past twenty years, in the Arab world, growth in per capita income was the lowest in the world except in sub-Saharan Africa. At an annual growth rate of 0.5 per cent annually, if such trends continued in the future, it would take the average Arab citizen 140 years to double his or her income, while other regions are set to achieve that level in a matter of less than ten years.

(ii) Labour productivity in the Arab world has been low and is declining. In fact:

(a) during 1960-1990, total factor productivity declined on an annual average of 0.2 per cent, while it rapidly accelerated in other parts of the world;

(b) compared to the Asian Tigers, in 1960, per capita output was higher than the average of this group; now it is half that of Korea;

(c) the productivity of Arab industrial labour in 1960 was 32 per cent that of the North American level; by 1990, it had fallen to 19 per cent.

(iii) The decline in workers' productivity has been accompanied by deterioration in real wages, which has accentuated poverty.

(iv) The report made it evident that, in both quantitative and qualitative terms the Middle East lagged far behind comparable regions in other parts of the world, and that, from a human development perspective, the state of human development in the Arab world is a cause for concern. Achievement by the Arab region on the *Human Development Index (HDI)* in the past decade was lower than the world average. Relative to other regions, the Arab world does better on income indicators than on development indicators. Thus, it can be said that the Arab region is richer than it is developed. Although income poverty is low compared to other parts of the world, the Arab region is hobbled by a different kind of poverty - *poverty of capabilities and poverty of opportunities.*

In conclusion, the report called for comprehensive reform in the Arab world; it said:

> The way forward involves tackling human capabilities and knowledge. *It also involves promoting systems of good governance,* those that promote, support and sustain human well-being, based on expanding human capabilities, choices, opportunities and freedoms (economic and social as well as political), especially for the currently poorest and most marginalised members of society. The empowerment of women must be fully addressed throughout. (Emphasis added.)

Even as the shocking findings of the report were being absorbed in the region, the Middle East was confronted with an aggressive American posture that included an assertion to pursue intrusive policies to "reform" the region in political, religious and social areas to neutralise the sources of Islam-based terror and to modernise Middle Eastern polities by imbuing them with the American virtues of freedom, democracy and free-markets. At the same time, the region's leaders and people watched helplessly and with alarm as, through 2002, the United States engaged in the harshest possible rhetoric against Iraq (as also, periodically, other countries in the region) and, by the end of the year, put in place diplomatic, political and logistical arrangements for armed assault on Iraq.

The Middle East Partnership Initiative

Amidst this military build-up, then Secretary of

State Colin Powell launched, on December 12, 2002, the US-Middle East Partnership Initiative [MEPI] to support development and reform projects in the Arab world. In his remarks before the Heritage Foundation, Powell drew a bleak picture of a region plagued by terrorist violence, anaemic economic growth, sharp differences between rich and poor, low representation of women in schools and the workplace, and a fast-rising and youthful population. He observed: " It has become increasingly clear that we must broaden our approach to the region (to) give sustained and energetic attention to economic, political and educational reform."[13]

Using facts from the AHDR, Powell pointed out that the combined GDP of 260m Arabs was less that of 40m Spaniards, and losing ground. He said Arab countries generated barely 1 per cent of the world's non-oil exports. Barely half of Arab women are literate, and had fewer representatives in parliaments than women of any other region. He also maintained that only one Arab in 100 has access to a computer. The new initiative, Powell noted, would spend $29m in its first year – and much more in later years – to work with Arab governments and civic organisations to close "the hope gap". [Allocation for fiscal 2003 was $100 million, and $90 million has been earmarked for fiscal 2004.][14]

The MEPI pursued many of the same types of political evolution, good governance, and civil society capacity-building projects which the Clinton administration had been content with, and at funding levels that were not dramatically higher. A close observer of US efforts to promote democracy in the Middle East during the Clinton years noted that:

> US efforts to promote Arab democracy seemed but an afterthought to the main objectives of US policy in the region. Pro-democracy initiatives remained at the level of "low policy", meaning that they were neglected or undermined at the more influential diplomatic level when they conflicted with core "high policy" interests such as regional security, oil and terrorism among others.[15]

The MEPI continued this tradition. It was to be handled by the State Department's Bureau of Near East Affairs. Its early work focused on programmes to promote literacy, expand computer use and Internet access, and foster women's involvement in politics and business. It also provided small loans for start-up business, and offered technical aid to Arab States seeking membership in the WTO. Powell in his remarks conceded that promoting democracy in the region would not be easy. Still, he added:

> We reject the condescending notion that freedom will not grow in the Middle East. Too many Middle Easterners are ruled by closed political systems, too many governments curb the institutions of civil society as a threat.[16]

The AHDR-2003

In October 2003, the second AHDR was published, again written by Arab intellectuals, think-tanks and NGOs, led by Nader Fergany.[17] In the preface, the authors averred that, since the publication of the earlier report, the challenges before Arab countries "remain critically pertinent and may have become even graver, especially in the area of freedom."[18] The authors affirmed that the second report would focus attention on the status of Arab knowledge: it was their finding that "disabling constraints hamper the acquisition, diffusion and production of knowledge in the Arab societies." According to the writers,

> Knowledge can help the region to expand the scope of human freedoms, enhance the capacity to guarantee those freedoms through good governance, and achieve the higher moral human goals of justice and human dignity. It also underlines the importance of knowledge to Arab countries as a powerful driver of economic growth through higher productivity.[19]

The authors expressed awareness of the political context in which their report was being published. They noted that:

> the region had recently encountered grave threats, and the dignity and rights of Arabs, especially the right to self-determination, have been grossly violated. Soon after the first Report was completed, Israel re-occupied the Palestinian territories. Barely one year later, Iraq fell under Anglo-American invasion and occupation. In these circumstances, the challenge of building Arab human development has undoubtedly become more perilous, certainly more arduous and possibly more tenuous.[20]

The authors also maintained that their findings could be misused or misinterpreted to serve the interests of parties within and outside the Arab world, "whose interests run counter to an Arab awakening". Still, the writers believed that "self-reform emerging from frank self-criticism was the correct and, perhaps, the only alternative to plans that are apparently being drawn up outside the Arab world for reconstructing the area and reshaping the Arab identity."[21] The authors concluded: "Turning a blind eye to the weaknesses and shortfall of the region, instead of decisively identifying and overcoming them, can only increase its vulnerability and leave it more exposed."[22]

The rest of the report provided a detailed critique of the state of the knowledge society in the Arab world. The report found serious obstacles to the knowledge dissemination process in Arab countries, and argued that, while there had been an impressive quantitative expansion of education in Arab countries in the second half of the 20th century, it was still modest compared with other developing countries, and included high rates of illiteracy among women and denial of access to basic education among children. Again, knowledge production in the region was meagre, particularly in the areas of science and technology and the "beleaguered" area of humanities.

The report noted that Arabic culture found itself facing the challenges of an emerging "global cultural homogeneity", and asserted that it had no choice but to engage in this "new global experiment."[23] The report was particularly critical of "political obstacles" to knowledge acquisition, which it saw as even more severe than those posed by socio-economic structures in the Arab countries. It pointed out that "oppression, the arbitrary application of laws, the selective censorship and other politically motivated restrictions" are widespread, all of which obstructed the diffusion of knowledge and education of public opinion.[24]

The "strategic vision" contained in the report for the establishment of a knowledge society in the Arab world was to be based on five pillars :[25]

i) guaranteeing the key freedoms of opinion, speech and assembly through good governance bounded by law;

ii) disseminating high quality education for all;

iii) embedding science and expanding the capacity for research and development in all societal activities;

iv) shifting rapidly towards knowledge based production in Arab socio-economic structures; and,

v) developing an authentic broad-minded and enlightened Arab knowledge model, which would entail :

   a) delivering true religion from political exploitation,

   b) advancing the Arabic language,

   c) reclaiming some of the bright spots in the Arab cultural heritage,

   d) promoting and celebrating cultural diversity, and,

   e) opening up to other cultures.

The two AHDRs provided the Bush Administration with the required data and impetus to articulate robustly a reform programme for the Middle East that would move beyond the modest goals of the Clinton Presidency and the State Department-led MEPI.

On November 6, 2003, President Bush, speaking before the National Endowment of Democracy in Washington, set out his grand vision for the reform of the Middle East. The President said :

> Sixty years of Western nations excusing and accommodating the lack of freedom in the Middle East did nothing to make us safe — because in the long run, stability cannot be purchased at the expense of liberty. *As long as the Middle East remains a place where freedom does not flourish, it will remain a place of stagnation, resentment, and violence ready for export.* And with the spread of weapons that can bring catastrophic harm to our country and to our friends, it would be reckless to accept the status quo. *Therefore, the US has adopted a new policy, a forward strategy of freedom in the Middle East.* This strategy requires the same persistence, energy and idealism we have shown before. And it will yield the same results. As in Europe, as in Asia, as in every region of the world, the advance of freedom leads to peace. (Emphasis added.)[26]

The stage was thus set for the presentation of a plan of action that would give substance to the President's vision and realise his "forward strategy of freedom."

II. The Greater Middle East Initiative (GMEI)

The "forward strategy of freedom in the Middle East," articulated by Bush in November 2003, was followed by the release, in February 2004, of an American "working paper" on the subject of Middle East reform which would be considered at the next G-8 Summit at Sea Island, Georgia, on June 8-10, 2004.* This paper was not officially published: it was leaked, and first printed in the London-based Saudi newspaper, *Al-Hayat*, on February 13, 2004.[1]

The paper described the "Greater Middle East" as the countries of the Arab world, and Pakistan, Afghanistan, Iran, Turkey and Israel. The paper began by recalling the findings of the two AHDRs relating to the three "deficits" in the Arab world pertaining to freedom, knowledge and women's empowerment. The paper warned that if the GMEI region were to continue on the same path, it would add every year to its population of "under-employed, under-educated and politically disenfranchised youth." This, according to the paper, would "pose a direct threat to the stability of the region and to the common interests of the G-8 members." The paper noted that the path of reform to be pursued would address the AHDR deficits by:

i) promoting democracy and good governance;

---

*Text at *Appendix I*

ii) building a knowledge society; and

iii) expanding economic opportunities.

The GMEI then provided a detailed action plan to address these reform priorities. Thus, in regard to *elections,* the G-8 promised to provide technical assistance in the management of elections at different levels as also for parliamentary exchanges and training. Similarly, towards building a *knowledge society,* the GMEI spoke of a basic education initiative which would include : literacy programmes, provision of textbooks, setting up of schools, and educational reform; the G-8 would be particularly active in the area of digital knowledge. Finally, with regard to expanding *economic opportunities,* the GMEI highlighted the need for an economic transformation in the region, focus on development of the private sector, and setting up of small and medium enterprises. Regarding *trade,* the G-8 members would commit themselves to providing WTO accession to the countries concerned, as also establishing trade hubs in the region and business incubator zones.

The US-based, Arab origin commentator, Shibley Telhami, who consulted with the Administration on the initiative, described it as the US government "looking beyond immediate trouble spots to institutionalise a policy of change for the region."[2] A State Department official thought that the initiative "would tear down the atrocities of [Islamic] extremism."[3] At the same time, he said, the Administration recognised the danger of "too rapid democratisation. We want to see steady progress over a period of time and we want to build in checks in the system."[4]

US/European Response

The publication of the GMEI created "a cottage industry" of comment in the US, Europe and the Arab world. Some American and European writers saw in the initiative an opportunity to bridge the Trans-atlantic divide created by the Iraq war. Others speculated whether the US would use NATO to promote the initiative in the region. In this context, they recalled that, in October 2003, the US Ambassador to NATO, Nicholas Burns, had told a conference in Prague :

> NATO's mandate is still to defend Europe and North America. But, we don't believe we can do that by sitting in Western Europe, or Central Europe, or North America. We have to deploy our conceptual attention and our military forces east and south. NATO's future, we believe, is east and south. It is in the Greater Middle East.[5]

Much of the American and European comment was critical of the initiative. Some felt that it was too modest and did not go far enough in pursuing the major reforms required in the region. Other writers were sceptical about the US interest in pushing through reform at the expense of its ties with its principal allies in the region; as one observer affirmed:

> It seems clear that the administration is unwilling to push the envelope and adopt a much more assertive policy towards non-democratic and largely non-reforming but friendly Middle Eastern states. Despite all the talk about a new paradigm for US

policy in the region, US policy makers are still effectively paralysed by an old problem : the clash between their stated desire for a deep-reaching transformation of the region and their underlying interest in maintaining the useful relations they have with the present governments of many non-democratic states there.[6]

A French political analyst conveyed the official French view that the initiative was deficient because it did not provide for a dialogue and partnership with the Arabs in evolving solutions to their predicament. The author quoted the former French Foreign Minister, Dominique De Villepin, as saying:

> It is essential to associate the countries involved with our own thoughts as much as possible, in the logic of a true partnership. One should avoid too uniformed an approach; countries in the Middle East are different; our approach should be global and take into consideration all political, economic, social, cultural and educational aspects.[7]

Villepin then proceeded to set out what in his view would have been the more suitable approach.

> Firstly, there should be political dialogue in order to make democracy, good governance and human rights move forward; secondly, there has to be economic and social development so as to implement the necessary structural reforms; lastly, supporting civil society in order to facilitate a dialogue between the cultures.[8]

The American commentator, Zbigniew Brzezinski, echoed this view.[9] He felt that the initiative had been unveiled by the President "in a patronising way", and was likely to evoke memories of French and British imperialism in the region. He also mentioned the omission in the GMEI of any reference to the resolution of the Arab-Israeli dispute, which would create the impression in the Arab world that democracy was the pre-condition to the addressing of this central issue. For the initiative to succeed, Brzezinski recommended the following:

(i) the initiative should be developed through discussion with the Arab countries;

(ii) it must be sensitive to the political dignity of the Arabs, which would be possible if the programme for democracy was matched by granting sovereignty to the Iraqis and Palestinians; and,

(iii) the US must define the substance of a peace settlement in the Middle East and work energetically to put it in place.

The British scholar, Fred Halliday, described the Middle East as a "tough neighbourhood that has hindered most progressive movements towards reform."[10] Regarding prospects for democracy in the Middle East, Halliday argued that democracy required four pre-conditions that did not at present exist in the Middle East:

(i) transparency in financial matters

(ii) right to vote

(iii) freedom of the Press

(iv) political institutions.

At the same time, Halliday applauded the "good changes" that had already occurred in the Gulf and observed that democracy would take time to be achieved. He advised that "we should be realistic and hopeful....we should have realistic goals and realistic assessment." He suggested Singapore as a good example for the Gulf to emulate – its economic achievement having been obtained "through education, with many tight technocratic elite pushing things forward."[11]

III. Response of the Arab World to the GMEI

The call for reform in the Arab world culminating in the publication of the GMEI has led to an extraordinary intellectual ferment in the region, with learned commentators filling hundreds of pages of editorial opinion.

Official Response and its Critics

The official response in the Arab world, particularly from principal Arab states like Egypt and Saudi Arabia, covered the following points:

(i) The timing for reform was not propitious: the Arab world was at war with Israel; the successful completion of that struggle required that its conduct be given full attention and not get diluted or distracted by other issues, which would only threaten the security and stability of the region.

(ii) There were differences in the political, economic and cultural situation in various Arab countries. Hence, the region could not be "reformed" through a single programme of action.

(iii) The dignity of the Arab world does not permit that we allow outsiders to intrude into our national setup and direct us as to how we should reform ourselves; we are fully capable of doing this on our own.

(iv) The political and social development of the people in most countries is at present so backward that in case free elections were to be held now, Islamic fundamentalists would be elected; they on coming to power would ensure that free elections are never held again. Hence, to avoid this regional and global catastrophe, the primary focus of our national effort at this stage should be on development other than freedom and political change.

However, these views are not shared by most Arab writers, liberal and conservative. There is broad consensus across the region that reform is urgently required. Several writers have spoken of the sense of hopelessness and despair across the Arab world, with the vast majority of people living under repressive and cruel autocracies, with little hope of any improvement in their situation or the retrieval of their dignity in the hostile environment in which they eke out their lives. One author spoke of the urgent need to introduce an era of Arab liberalism so that it would inject into the prevailing Arab system "transparency, the rule of law and freedom as pillars of free civil society", and thus "expose the emptiness of fundamentalist thinking".[1]

The Egyptian Islamist, Fahmi Huweidi, noted that, in certain Arab quarters, the "atmosphere of defeat" was so intense that some people even favoured an American occupation. He described such persons as "desperate and broken people" who had become so dejected that "they were ready to make a pact with a devil, if that will bring them deliverance." He concluded that if the Arabs wished to avoid foreign intervention in their affairs and the threat of violence from extremists, it was essential that they "open up choices for peaceful changes within".[2]

The Lebanese writer, Satie Noureddin, harshly criticised the position of Arab governments to reform. Referring to it as "an unbelievable amount of mutual duplicity and hypocrisy," he commented acerbically:

> The arguments deployed in this dispute reveal an unfamiliar level of patriotism, chivalry, valour, and heroism: Total Arab concern for preserving sovereignty, independence, and freedom of Arab decision-making, and a rejection of all forms of foreign intervention in internal affairs. It is a movement of resistance to a US-led assault on Arab values, traditions, and culture, and a campaign to confront the onslaught against the Arabs' Islamic identity.[3]

According to another Lebanese writer, the Arab regimes had attempted to beguile their population with offers of economic benefit in place of freedom and democracy. Now, however, the defeat of Saddam's Iraq and the occupation of the largest Arab state, has sent a harsh message to the effect that "the time of illusory victories has come to an end, and that full bellies are not enough to lift people up from despondency, despair, and the resort to violence."[4]

Salameh Neemat in the *Al-Hayat*, asked whether

the Arab States from the Atlantic Ocean to the Arabian Gulf were actually engaged in a real military war with Israel. He maintained that the Arab regimes have been preoccupied with repressing their peoples who sought democracy "after these very same regimes failed to confront Israel for reasons that included the fact that they are undemocratic. Now, Arab officials are telling us that they reject the imposition of democracy from outside, as if they were ever ready to respond to the demands for democracy from within."[5]

On the same lines, another writer, Abdelmoneim Said, writing in the Saudi-based *Al-Watan*, said: "It is both morally and politically wiser to disengage the issue of reform from the Arab-Israeli conflict." He asserted firmly: "the rights of Arab citizens should not be held hostage to any cause, no matter how noble important or central it might be."[6]

The Lebanese writer, Hussam Itani, responded with the fiercest anger to the regimes rejecting reform on the ground that it is foreign-imposed. He said:

> Prohibition and self-imposed abstention from any real criticism of the prevailing consciousness has turned superficiality into the highest degree of creativity, vileness into the highest form of politics, and dependence as the fastest way to catch up with modernity. Despite all this, some have emerged to preach 'the middle-ground' as the magic word and the cure-all for our malaise.[7]

One of the most effective attacks on the regimes that oppose reform has come from the distinguished Lebanese commentator Joseph Samaha.[8] Responding to the assertions that the reform initiative is imposed from outside and that priority should be given to the settlement of the conflict with Israel, Samaha observed:

(i) There is an apparent contradiction in the position of the Arab regimes which, on the one hand, reject foreign reform in the name of sovereignty but, on the other hand, beg for foreign intervention to settle their conflict with Israel.

(ii) By rejecting reform until there is an Arab-Israeli settlement is in effect a directive to the outsider [USA] "to ensure that it does not commit the mistake of releasing (popular) forces that are opposed to it and the regimes that are subordinated to it."

(iii) The contention that reform has been rejected (by Arab leaders) because it is imported from abroad is false. The factual position is that what is being rejected is the reform that is being demanded internally, and that may sometimes imply serious change.

Salahuddin Hafiz, writing in *Al-Ahram*,[9] accepted that societies and states have particularities and different circumstances which would lead to different programmes and priorities for reform. Still, he asserted, "there are certain internationally accepted yardsticks for democratic reform." In this regard, he set out the following:

(i) public and personal freedoms

(ii) rotation of power and popular participation

(iii) popular elections

(iv) freedom to political parties

(v) just laws and independent judiciary

(vi) press freedom

(vii) safeguard and preserve human rights

(viii) abrogation of emergency laws and courts

(ix) genuine economic reform

(x) fundamental changes in education curriculum, culture and media to promote opening up to contemporary culture and acceptance of science and technology.

Questions about US Credibility

Though there was a consensus on the need for reform and a general rejection of the opposition voiced by the regimes, the American authorship of the GMEI made its credentials suspect in the eyes of several commentators. The main points made by them in this regard were:

(i) The US's primary interests in the Middle East have been to protect the region's oil resources and guarantee the free flow of oil to the West at acceptable prices, and the security of Israel. In pursuit of these interests, the United States has supported the most authoritarian and repressive regimes. Thus, it must accept a considerable portion of responsibility for the present malaise in the Middle East.

(ii) The United States is now promoting "reform" in the Middle East in pursuit of its strategic interest which, at present, following the events of September 11, is defined as the "war on terrorism". However, in pursuing this line, the United States has wilfully ignored its own role in the emergence of present-day Islamic extremism and global *jihad*.

(iii) Given its record, the USA has no "moral authority" to preach or promote reform in the Arab world. It has contributed to the anger and despair of the Arabs on account of its uneven-handed approach to the Arab-Israeli issue, which finds absolutely no mention in the GMEI.

(iv) The present US administration is dominated by pro-Israeli rightwing neocons who have a substantial record of hostility to the Arab interest. Arab liberals would be reluctant to associate themselves with such a rightwing Administration.

(v) The USA is not sincere about promoting reform in the Arab world. Its primary interests in the region are strategic; reform will lead to the end of the existing pro-US regimes so that new leaderships would emerge that would

> genuinely serve Arab interests. The GMEI is thus a case of "political grand-standing" with electoral considerations to make up for the Iraq disasters and the failure in the war on terror.

Several writers were suspicious of the territorial grouping included in the initiative. Khaled Hroub did not believe it was an "innocent configuration" and saw in it "a new approach to the region's political geography".[10] He thought the initiative was based on the assumption that "the region is pregnant with political, security and social crises" and that it "exports crises to the world." However, Hroub was unable to understand how the USA, in its diagnosis, entirely failed to mention the contribution of Israel to this situation, which had drained the region of its energy and wealth as a result of its ongoing wars of aggression. He noted that the region had also suffered "the worst forms of foreign intervention and direct and indirect Western colonialisation over the last two centuries" whose adverse impact had continued with the creation of the State of Israel. Again, the discovery of oil resources had encouraged Western interventionist policies in the region, with the attendant propping up of repressive regimes and the consequent denial to the people of freedom, human rights, equal economic rights and good governance.

The Pakistani writer, Mushahid Hussain, affirmed that there was every reason to suspect that the initiative was motivated by US strategic interests, and pointed out that the territory included in it "also happens to be the operational responsibility of the US Central Command [CENTCON], which is militarily spearheading the 'war on terror'."[11] Nasim Zehra criticised the inclusion of Pakistan in the GMEI, arguing that it is not a Middle Eastern country, and nor does it require "the political and economic reforms of the scale that may be required by some of the Middle Eastern States."[12]

A number of Arab writers questioned the seriousness of the US's commitment to reform and democracy in the "Greater Middle East". Clovis Maksoud , the prominent Arab intellectual and one of the authors of AHDR-2003, confirmed the widespread impression in the Arab world that the US "wanted to establish what they called 'reforms' in their geopolitical interests, rather than responding to the fundamental requirements and needs of the Arab people."[13] The Jordanian writer, Hasan Abu Nimah, saw in the initiative a dark US conspiracy which was "the wiping out of the Arab position towards Israel by creating a domesticated generation and tamed regimes (not necessarily newly elected ones) who would drop every claim against Israel....the veiled intention of the reform (is) to end the conflict without resolving it."[14]

Khaled Hroub expressed the same suspicion of the US's sincerity in promoting the reform initiative.[15] In this context, he noted:

> the unrivalled US / Western zeal to establish strong relations with the regional regimes that were earlier classified as 'rogue', and that bear no relation whatsoever to democracy ...in return for their

abandonment of 'on-paper' weapons of mass destruction and their cooperation with Washington in 'the war on terrorism'.

It is as if Washington is assuming that the criterion of good governance is to abandon armament programmes, and not to promote democracy and respect for human rights.

Said Al-Shihabi was more specific in his criticism of the US's double standards. He noted that "Washington has been pursuing highly selective policies that do not distinguish between interests and principles", and in fact favour the former over the latter. He illustrated this by pointing out that Bush had readily "chastised Iran for its lack of democracy, while lauding Saudi Arabia's 'readiness to' implement reforms." Similarly, Bater Mohammed Ali Wardam noted that the USA:

> has rushed to open up to Libya after the Libyan leadership announced an end to its armament programmes and its readiness to open its files on Islamic opposition figures and organisations that it supported in the past to the CIA. In this context...Washington has said nothing about the need for good governance in Libya.[17]

The Editor-in-Chief of *Gulf News*, Abdul Hamid Ahmad, castigated the United States for the miserable Arab situation:

> These people [the Arabs] are still paying the price for such [US] policies – they are frustrated at the failure to resolve the Palestinian issue, economic and social backwardness, lack of development projects, growing unemployment and illiteracy. And, above

all, the basic principles of human rights do not exist. The result is that there is no freedom, no public participation in the political realm and no free media.[18]

It is interesting to note that one of the severest attacks on the US initiative has come from Nader Fergany, the lead author of the two AHDRs. Fergany's criticism focused on the selective use of material from the reports, thus deliberately excluding some of its important points relating to the causes of the Arab predicament as also the remedial action suggested.[19] Regarding the former, Fergany emphasised the US responsibility for the human development crisis in the region. He specifically referred to:

(i) unconditional US support to Israel in violation of fundamental Arab rights to liberty and self-determination;

(ii) support to repressive regimes in the region "as long as they serve your interests at the expense of their citizens"; and,

(iii) the US invasion of Iraq, which "will not further human development in the Arab region, as exactly in the same way that the death of nearly half a million Iraqi children as a result of the sanctions regime did not further human development in the region."

Referring to the intrusive character of the US initiative, Fergany said:

Intervention from outside deprives Arabs of their

fundamental right to self-determination....The essence of human development is unleashing the creative potential of people in the region, not supplanting it by misguided intervention from outside.[20]

In response to GMEI's frequent reliance on the AHDRs, Fergany caustically observed this was "like a drunk leans against a lamppost so he does not fall over, and not for illumination."[21]

When the Abu Ghraib abuses were revealed, Fergany was firmly convinced that the USA could not be the harbinger of reform in the Middle East. He said:

The US administration must atone for its sins against the entire Arab nation, must make up for its violations of the legitimate rights of our people in Palestine and Iraq. The crimes of the current US administration are so diverse and inexcusable that it would take perseverance and creativity, over a long span of time, to make things good.

Obviously, the US administration is not going to consider atoning for its crimes unless the Arabs, nations and governments, take action beyond anger and denunciation, unless they do something to fight off imperialism, unless they start boycotting products and harming US interests.

To those Arabs who dream of freedom at the hands of the Americans, I have this to say: Look at what is happening to the Iraqis.[22]

Another commentator noted that, while pursuing democracy in the Middle East, the United States "has yet to state its position regarding the region's many dictatorships."[23] The writer's principal concern was that the USA continues to value its ties with such regimes over all other considerations; he concluded: "Democracy cannot succeed unless there is a complete divorce with oppressive and tyrannical regimes."

Albadr Alshateri accepted this analysis and asserted that "Bush is not about to trade friendly regimes with hostile democrats. Better an Arab satrap than an Arab Chirac."[24] The author concluded:

> Arab regimes, who by now are masters of razzmatazz and specious thinking, would give Bush what he wants, a sham of democracy and a foisted representative government to duck what they believe is a coming storm.
>
> Unbeknownst to them, however, what they are actually ducking is no storm; it is a bubble that will burst on US rock solid strategic interests.

Other voices, while accepting that the USA is not a credible promoter of reform, have recommended that reforms should not be rejected only because they have emerged as a result of an American initiative. The *Gulf News* in its editorial pointed out that, for decades the people of the Arab world had been fed promises of reform, but this was something "they have not tasted so far, thanks to the lack of foresight and commonsense from the parties involved." Now that Americans have decided to urge reforms, the initiative "should not be criticised or rejected pointblank." Instead, according to the paper, the Arab world "should shoulder the responsibility of asking itself what alternatives it has if it does not reform." That the Arab Foreign Ministers in Cairo [March 2004] had failed to finalise a joint plan for reform proved that " there exists a bankruptcy in churning out fresh ideas and plans on the issue of reform."[25]

Abdul Hamid Ahmad, the *Gulf News* editor, also pointed out that, over the last 50 years, Arab regimes had always been pro-American. Similarly, the US had always vehemently supported Arab regimes which "worked against the wishes and aspirations of their peoples striving for a better life." Referring to this as an "unholy alliance", Ahmad argued that, as a result, the people were the sole losers. However, now when the American ally of the Arab regimes has suggested a reform programme, the regimes have severely opposed it. This is not surprising because it includes ensuring "the rule of law, public institutions, freedom and political participation." Arab regimes have continuously denied these demands, raising again the slogans of war against Israel. This, in the view of the editor, is "shameful, political blackmail."[26]

Yasser Zaatra, in Jordan's *Al-Dustour*, believed that neither the USA nor the Arab regimes were sincere about reform. He said: "No one wants real reform…It is safe to bet that not a single Arab regime that talks about reform is seeking a peaceful rotation of power, full freedom of expression, real protection of civil society…." But, in Zaatra's view, the Arab predicament was even more acute. Given the US record in the region, he accepted that "it is only normal for Arab citizens to feel sympathetic towards opponents of reform as demanded by the United States, even when they realise that the opponents of this kind of reform are also opponents of reform in its real and desirable sense." The central dilemma was:

> the fact that all are equally opposed to real reform allows those (leaders) who reject American diktats to be closer to the spirit of the masses, even when the Arab masses may also be opposed to some of their [leaders'] policies.[27]

Ramzy Baroud clarified the Arab dilemma in the clearest terms when he said:

> It seems that while many Arabs distrust the US government policies in the region, they don't reject the concept of reform at hand; they simply hope that their leaders would be prudent enough to espouse internal reforms that cater to the individual Arab, rather than to merely attempt to secure its turf from the uninvited American intervention in their affirs....*Arab governments are capable of negotiating their way out of the reform debacle, through well-examined concessions, most likely made to US interests* and to the interests of its favourite regional ally, Israel. *The US government is equally capable of rearranging – or renaming its priorities – in the Middle East*, with unbinding cosmetic assertions. (Emphasis added)[28]

Obstructions to Reform: Despair and Optimism

A number of writers have noted that, while there is an urgent need for reform in the Arab world, beyond the reluctance of the principal regimes there are other serious obstructions to the implementation of the reform proposals. Thus, Abdelwahab el-Effendi has affirmed that democracy "cannot secure a foothold in societies that do not have strong democratic movements....The Arab and Islamic elite have failed to create such movements so far."[29] Another writer, Mohammad Ibrahim, writing in *Al-Nahar*, argues that local forces that support change are still in their infancy, while existing regimes continue to be obstacles to development and democracy.[30]

Indeed, seeing the objective situation, the Kuwaiti, writer Nazim Shafik al-Ghabra, struck a note of despair when he said:

> The Arab world is ready for reform neither in the cultural and educational sphere, nor in the political and economic sphere, nor in the social sphere. Moreover, the Arab states are unsure about what sort of reform they want to bring about through the changes they are trying to implement....

Reform requires reformists; it requires reformist forces in society; and it requires more than a presidential decision made today only to be cancelled tomorrow.[31]

It is interesting to note that, in contrast to the pessimism and even despair apparent in a few writers, several liberal commentators, particularly in Saudi Arabia, are very pleased at what has been achieved so far and remain optimistic about the future. Referring to the Saudi government's announcement of municipal elections in early 2005, the Saudi scholar, Ghazi Al-Maghlooth, said:

> Be that as it may, at this stage, it is enough that the word "elections" has entered the Saudi vocabulary, and that the concept of elections has been embedded into the conceptual mindset of our Saudi society, and that the stagnant waters of our national life have been stirred. For too long, we have been living in a state of frozen, rock-solid rigidity day in and day out.

Elections are surely not a goal in themselves, but for us, at this stage, they are. We need to consolidate this culture into our collective mind, and cultivate it to harvest its fruits in the future. The municipal sector is probably a good place to start to involve people in local decision-making, especially that municipal services have a direct effect on people's lives.[32]

Similarly, referring to the proposed Saudi municipal elections, the Lebanese writer, Sati'e Noureddin, described them as a "Half-a-step forward in the one-thousand-mile journey to political and social reform".[33] He believed that the elections "consolidated the principle of resorting to the ballot box which is one of the main pillars of modernity." The elections signify:

that the [Saudi] ruling family now needs greater popular participation in the administration of a society that is moving at high speed.

It also suggests that the Saudi political forces are now invited to emerge from the shade and from the realm of semi-secret statements and petitions in order to engage in an experiment that is the first of its kind in the history of the Kingdom. In this sense the decision to hold these elections can be seen as a decisive turning point.

The liberal Saudi commentator, Turki al-Hamad, saw in the election announcement "a new way of thinking ...tantamount to a systemic revolution in Saudi political thinking and in the philosophy of the Government in the Kingdom." He concluded:

The mere fact that terms such as 'mass participation,' 'elections,' and 'widened public participation' are

> being used is extremely significant. It is not important whether or not the Saudi leadership is really persuaded that this is the right way to go. What is important is that the survival of the Saudi state is at risk; this is enough to persuade Saudi leaders to adopt change.
>
> With the measures announced last week, Saudi decision makers...broke down the psychological barriers between Saudis and the current age, democracy, rational thinking and – most important of all – they tore down the barriers that prevented ordinary Saudis from seeing the interests of their country as being supreme.[34]

The Lebanese writer, Ali Hamadeh, castigated the Arab regimes for their continued supineness in the face of external pressures. He said: "They [Arab regimes] did not remember the poor, destitute and crushed Arab public except when colonialism returned through the widest portals back to the beating heart of Arabism." Still, he was convinced that this official Arab weakness would no longer continue since popular opinion had decided to resist it. He asserted:

> The official Arab system has been defeated. Nothing remains of it except its intelligence arms, and a popular fear that is has almost become second nature in the Arab world. The fear is of the excessive 'courage' of the Arab police in defending their regimes, the regimes of shared benefits–nay, the Mafioso regimes that have only been built on blood, and that will not fall before the poor and destitute Arab public dares to say 'No!'
>
> Once it does this, we will produce a proud public

that will prevent the official Arab system from riding the wave of reform and, on the pretext of reform, remain in charge of the process of reform for another hundred years.[35]

IV. Official Arab Reform Initiatives

In response to the US assertions on the need to reform the region, but particularly after the publication of the GMEI, efforts were made in certain Arab capitals to develop indigenous reform plans which would be sensitive to the situation in the countries of the region. One of the important initiatives in this regard was the meeting of Egyptian intellectuals at Alexandria. According to press reports, this was a "counter-initiative" launched by Egypt: it was in keeping with President Mubarak's rejection of any effort to impose foreign cultural models for change and his insistence on indigenous initiatives that would respect Arab identities, and proceed at a pace that would be in keeping with their own situation.[1] Saudi Arabia explicitly joined Egypt in this rejection of the GMEI; a joint Saudi-Egyptian statement issued in Riyadh after Mubarak's visit on February 24, 2004, asserted: "Arab states (would) proceed on the path of development, modernisation and reform in keeping with their people's interests and values."[2]

The meeting at Alexandria Library took place in the second week of March 2004, under the banner: "Arab Reform Issues: Vision and Implementation". In a sharp criticism of the handling of this initiative, Ayman Sharaf maintained that the three-day conference was announced only a few days before it began; it was restricted to a few people, and all the sessions were closed to the public and media. Many of those in attendance were close to their ruling regimes and there were hardly any government critics present.[3]

President Mubarak addressed the conference's opening session on March 12, when he said :

> This conference on Arab reforms gains significance for many considerations as it is held upon a self-initiative by a number of non-governmental organisations and businessmen councils that represent the broadest possible sector of specialists, researchers and those who are interested in Arab affairs.[4]

The Alexandria conference's agenda was quite similar to the US-initiative in calling for promoting democracy, knowledge society and economic opportunities. The measures recommended include: expanding popular participation in democratic political practices; encouraging pluralism; stopping intervention in elections, and abolishing restrictions on speech. On the economic level, the recommendations call for accelerating the elimination of restrictions on capital movement between Arab countries and amending tax and duty laws. Arab governments are invited to expand social security networks, upgrade health services and develop education programmes.[5]

Besides the Alexandria conference, there were other government-sponsored conferences of Arab NGOs and business communities. The meeting at *Sanaa* took place earlier, on January 10-12, 2004; it was organised by the government and the Yemeni NGO, "No Peace Without

Justice." It had several hundred participants from 52 countries. It issued the "Declaration on Democracy, Human Rights and the Role of the International Criminal Court," which affirmed the following:[6]

(i) democracy and human rights, which have their origin in faith and culture, are interdependent and inseparable,

(ii) need for dialogue and understanding to bridge cultural and religious diversity,

(iii) democratic values and institutions to be set up/strengthened,

(iv) need to promote rule of law, free and independent media, development of civil society, and the development of the private sector.

This was followed by the publication of the *blueprint of the Amman-based Arab Business Council* which called for economic liberalisation, good governance and human development. It also called upon Arab leaders to seize the opportunity of the WEF convened at Amman, between May 15-17, 2004, "to leverage regional and international partnerships to forge a stable future for the region."[7]

Finally, on the eve of the G-8 meeting, a conference on "Democracy and Reform in the Arab World" took place in *Doha* on June 3-4, 2004. In his inaugural address,[8] the Amir of Qatar, Sheikh Hamad bin Khalifa Al-Thani, firmly rejected the various reasons presented (by Arab leaders) to avoid or postpone reform.

Referring to the contention that there were differences and disparities among Arab countries which justified a different prescription for each country, the Amir pointed out that there was "a common denomination of reforms (which) has to be implemented by all."

Referring to the criticism that reforms urged from outside were not acceptable, the Amir said that "the [Arab] nation did not pay attention [to reform] in the right time, so it suffers today.... While the region, due to its delay, has encouraged outsiders to offer proposals and initiative for reform, its enlightened nationals remain the most capable of formulating an independent Arab reformatory vision." The Amir called for:

(i) deeper Arab engagement with the outside world;

(ii) a new culture that replaces the culture of dominance and oppression;

(iii) the need to fight corruption and consolidate transparency; and

(iv) the need to revive the spirit of true religion that upholds democracy.

The Tunis Declaration

In March 2004, a few weeks after the "leak" of the GMEI, Arab leaders were still overwhelmed by this robust US intervention in their polity: not surprisingly, they were deeply divided in their response, with some North African and Gulf countries, with Jordan, advocating a positive response, while Egypt, Syria and

Saudi Arabia fiercely opposed this intrusive agenda. However, finally, when the Arab League Summit reconvened in Tunis on May 22-23, 2004, the leaders did agree on a reform plan in the shape of the "Tunis Declaration."[9] The Declaration, in its first few clauses, addressed the Arab-Israeli conflict, the protection of the Palestinian people and the sovereignty and territorial integrity of Iraq.*

The second part of the Declaration, consisting of 11 sub-clauses, set out the commitment to reform of the Arab leaders; they agreed to:

i) uphold human rights,

ii) carry on reform in their countries "to keep pace with the accelerated world changes through the consolidation of democratic practices, the broadening of participation in political and public life and the reinforcement of the role of all components of civil society, including the non-governmental organisations in conceiving the guidelines of the society of tomorrow,"

iii) widen women's participation in the political, economic, social, cultural and educational fields, reinforce their rights and their position in society, and carry on promoting family and the protection of Arab youth,

iv) upgrade education and enhance knowledge,

---

*Text at *Appendix II*

v) promote economic cooperation,

vi) promote solidarity and mutual aid between Arab states,

vii) promote cooperation in the areas of communications and IT,

viii) promote dialogue between the religions and cultures, and,

ix) fight all forms of terrorism.

V. GMEI Revised: The Broader Middle East and North Africa Partnership [BMEP]

The meeting of the G-8 at Sea Island, Georgia, between June 8-10, 2004, to consider the GMEI, included the Heads of State from the following Islamic countries: Afghanistan, Algeria, Bahrain, Jordan, Turkey, Yemen and Iraq. [Egypt, Saudi Arabia, Morocco and Tunisia declined the invitation; Qatar was not invited owing to American unhappiness regarding the role being played by Al Jazeera television in "promoting terrorism".] From this meeting emerged the "Broader Middle East/ North Africa Partnership" [BMEP] document[1] which provided for "Partnership for Progress and a Common Future with the Region of the Broader Middle East and North Africa." *This was a revised version of the GMEI, based on the feedback received by American officials from European and Arab interlocutors.[2] The changes included:

i) The adjective "Greater" was dropped at the instance of some European countries who felt that it had unsavoury associations with military/imperialist expansionism; accordingly, it was replaced by the term "Broader".

ii) The GMEI in a footnote had specified the

---

*Text at *Appendix III*

geographical coverage of the territory covered by the initiative; now, in the BMEP, the territory was not specified. Before the G-8 Meeting, Under Secretary of State Allen Larson, in his Senate testimony, on June 2, 2004, had clarified:

> We believe that it is important to have an open architecture on a concept like this because we found in other regional organisations that when it's successful, others want to join. So we have not wanted to draw very sharp lines, excluding some and including others. But we certainly imagine the countries of North Africa, the Levant and the Gulf and some adjacent countries. We think that the geography will vary somewhat depending on the topics under discussion.[3]

iii) In the introductory part of the BMEP text, of the earlier negative references to the state of the Arab world, derived from the AHDRs, were removed. These were replaced by a positive reference to the region's "rich tradition and culture of accomplishment in government, trade, science, the arts and more. They have made many lasting contributions to human civilisation."

iv) The statement declared unequivocally that "successful reform depends on the countries in the region and change should not and cannot be imposed from outside." In order to affirm that the reform programme was not being enforced from outside, the BMEP, throughout its text, quoted extensively from the recommendations of earlier Arab conferences advocating reform, such as the Tunis Declaration, and the NGO Conferences of Alexandria, Sana'a and Amman.

v) The partnership now included detailed references to the two political issues of deep concern to the region : the Arab-Israeli conflict and Iraq; it noted that while "regional conflicts must not be an obstacle for reforms," the resolution of "long-lasting, often bitter, disputes, especially the Israeli-Palestinian conflict, is an important element of progress in the region." In this regard, "our support for reform in the region will go hand in hand with our support for a just, comprehensive and lasting settlement to the Arab-Israeli conflict, based upon UN Resolutions 242 and 338."

The BMEP had a separate action plan titled : "G-8 Plan of Support for Reform".[4] This action plan provided for an institutional arrangement to implement the partnership, i.e. the Forum for the Future, at which governments and business and civil society leaders would meet regularly to discuss reform goals and programmes.*

The rest of the plan referred to efforts to promote the following:

(a) Micro-finance arrangements

---

*Text at *Appendix III*

(b) literacy

(c) entrepreneurship and vocational training

(d) enterprise development

(e) training to promote free and transparent elections

(f) support to parliamentary exchange and training

(g) democracy assistance dialogue under the "Forum for the Future"

(h) expansion of women's participation in various fields and enhancement of their rights and status

(i) judicial reforms

(j) free expression and independent media

(k) good governance, transparency and anti-corruption efforts

(l) reforming the educational systems

(m) accelerating employment opportunities

(n) vocational training

(o) development of small and medium enterprises; promotion of investment; promotion of intra-regional trade and expansion of trade in global markets.

Observers have noted that the BMEP is "almost

totally different from what the Americans originally had in mind."[5] They maintain that the influence of G-8 leaders on Bush was particularly important. Thus, President Chirac is said to have told the Sea Island gathering that "there is no ready-made formula for democracy readily transposable from one country to another. Democracy is not a method, it is a culture. For democracy to take root solidly and durably in the Arab world, it must be an Arab democracy before all else." The French President also argued that only by restarting the peace process and de-escalating the level of violence in the region will the G8 "be able to dispel the hostility towards the West which is so widespread in the Middle East."

Critics have observed that the BMEP is not only "a considerable climbdown" from the lofty ambitions proclaimed by President Bush in his November 2003 speech, it is also a "drastic narrowing of the initial goals" set out in the original GMEI.[7] Commentators believe that the old GMEI has now:

> become a victim of the administration's other failures: of the growing violence in Iraq; the accumulated poison in transatlantic relations, and the backlash to Mr. Bush's decision to endorse Israel's unilateral redrawing of its borders.[8]

Michael Young, a convert to Islam, and opinion editor of the Beirut-based, *Daily Star*, has deeply regretted that, while finalising the Partnership, the USA "caved in to Arab and European pressures", and formulated "a far more anaemic plan".[9] He was unhappy that the shortcomings in the Arab world set out in the GMEI (based on the AHDRs) had now been omitted. More seriously, a document that had earlier projected Arab reform as a Western national security requirement had now been watered down to "a blueprint for a consensual and interactive process". In this "neutering" of the American plan, he saw the contribution of the Europeans; he quoted a European official as saying:

> This started as an American initiative, but I think we have managed to shape it in a way which is very much in line with our own ideas concerning how to deal with the Middle East region.... Essentially, it is based on the idea of partnership and dialogue, on the need for long-term engagement, the idea that there is no 'one-size-fits-all' approach.[10]

Young regretted that Europe had thus defeated "the only serious effort made in the last half-century to open up the Arab world."

Tamara Wittes, a regular commentator on Middle East reform, saw in the BMEP far-reaching American compromises to obtain the endorsements of other powers for US policy in Iraq and on Middle East reform. Wittes felt the new document was "long on declaratory rhetoric and short on meaningful steps to promote democracy in the region".[11] However, she accepted that the "Forum for the Future", by including the business sector and civil society as "full partners" in the reform process (with governments), did provide an opportunity to Arab reformers to pursue their agenda.

She regretted, however, that the BMEP did not have the capacity to "persuade" Arab autocrats to loosen domestic controls, and also did not provide for human rights criteria for participating in the various developmental programmes envisaged in the Partnership. This, she feared, would enable Arab States to pursue economic reforms while ignoring the political reforms they were not keen on. Overall, Wittes believed that the West has accepted Arab terms of "local ownership, diversity of approaches and the central importance of resolving the Israeli-Palestinian conflict." At the same time, she felt that, through participation in the Forum of the Future, private Arab citizens had obtained a unique opportunity to influence the foreign policies of Western governments in areas of crucial importance to them.

The response to the BMEP in the Arab world has been predictably mixed. Editorial comment reflecting official opinion is positive, while liberal writers are appalled and severely critical of what has emerged from South Island, Georgia. Reflecting the former view, the editorial in the Saudi daily, *Al Watan*, welcomed the BMEP but not for its promotion of reform which, according to the paper, the countries of the region already recognised the need for and had begun to implement various programmes in accordance with their "religious, social and cultural nature of their societies."[12] According to the paper, the two positive features of the Partnership were that reform would not be imposed from outside and, more significantly, the resolution of the Arab-Israeli conflict was now given due importance. The paper said that the settlement of this conflict would actually improve the response of

Arab society to reform proposals since, in the absence of such a resolution, the region viewed reforms negatively, seeing them as imposed from outside even when they emerged from within! The paper concluded:

> Once such a settlement finds its way to realisation, it will become the lightning rod for real reforms in the future. Without such a rod, all reforms will remain half-hearted and incomplete, and the Arab states will find it impossible to proceed with their reform programmes standing on one leg alone.

The response of Arab liberals has been quite different. Abdelwahab el-Effendi saw in the BMEP a victory of the Arab regimes.[13] According to him, political reform was "born lame and unable to stand on its own feet, and democratic progress has been made dependent on consultations with the very same ruler it is meant to replace." Effendi saw the action plan of the BMEP as grossly inadequate and "an insult and an affront to Arab democrats and Arab people." He concluded:

> The problem is not that the Arabs are illiterate and need to be educated, or poor and need loans, or ignorant and need someone to teach them what democracy is.
>
> The problem is that there are carnivorous monsters that will not permit anything to grow and develop in this Arab jungle....
>
> If the Arab world needs help, then the help it dreams of is of the kind that will help it in its battle to topple and get rid of these savage regimes.

The liberal writer Joseph Samaha saw in the BMEP

"a match between modesty and collusion".[14] According to Samaha, the American approach was "modest" as a result of the "disruption of its Iraqi adventure" because of which it was now moving towards pluralism and seeking compromises at the United Nations. "Collusion" was what the Arab leaders were engaged in: supporting US interests in regard to oil production; cooperation with Sharon and in the war of terror; supporting US activity in Iraq, and promising educational reforms. In this coming together of modesty and collusion, "there is no sign of any reformist measure". Instead, there is an increase in "the official Arab system's subservience to the United States, and the beginning of the realisation of the conditions necessary for withdrawing the reformist clause from the agenda."

The Lebanese writer Ramzi Baroud also saw a nexus between US interests and those of Arab leaders in going slow on reform. According to him:

> Middle East reform is a play out of self-centred values, be it strategic, economic or political. What has been almost completely discounted is the plight of those whose welfare should have been kept in the forefront of any sincere democratic change: The disfranchised, largely unemployed and freedom-deprived Arab masses.
>
> If such reconciliation of interests [between the USA and Arab leaders] – which seems to be the case – defined the current reforms legacy in the Middle East, the ultimate beneficiary of genuine democratic reform, the people of the region, will become its ultimate fatality. Then, no matter what it's called,

> the "Greater Middle East" will remain a euphemism for greater political stagnation, injustice and imperial designs.[15]

The Egyptian leftwing intellectual, Sherif Hetata, saw the BMEP's emphasis on economic reform as part of the principal Western interest to pursue its economic agenda in the region.[16] According to Hetata, there is a "fundamental contradiction" between the Western agenda of privatisation and de-industrialisation and the democratic aspirations of the people. He felt that Arab leaders were colluding with Western countries in the area of economic "reform" so that they could obtain "more space of manoeuvre for themselves" and "remain in the saddle of a mount which threatens to unseat at any moment."

The Rabat Conference: Meeting of the "Forum for the Future"

The various issues pertaining to reform in the Arab world came to the fore when the first meeting of the "Forum for the Future", envisaged in the Broader Middle East and North Africa Partnership, took place in Rabat on December 11-12, 2004. Well before the Conference, the *New York Times* reported that the Americans "have no plans to introduce any political initiatives to encourage democratic change."[17] The paper elaborated: "The popular view of the United States in the region has grown so dark, even hateful, that American officials are approaching the [Rabat] meeting with caution and with a package of financial and social initiatives that have only a scant relationship to the original goal of political change."

On the eve of the Conference, at a media briefing, the US Under Secretary of State for Economic, Business and Agricultural Affairs confirmed the cautious and moderate American approach when he said that the Conference was intended "to create greater opportunities for the next generation in the broader Middle East" through grants and aid to small businesses, networking among regional financial institutions and exchanging "views about how to bring more capital in the region," among other ideas.[18]

The Rabat Conference was attended by Foreign, Finance and Economy Ministers of 28 countries, including several Arab countries, representatives of the G-8, the European Union, Pakistan, Turkey and Afghanistan. Civil societies and business leaders also participated in the Forum. As expected, Arab leaders emphasised the need for political solutions to ongoing regional issues as a prelude to serious political and economic reform. Saudi Foreign Minister Saud Al Faisal said: "Let us face it... the real bone of contention is the longest conflict in modern history. For too long, the Arabs have witnessed the Western bias towards Israel."[19]

Amr Moussa, the Secretary General of the Arab League, echoed this view and linked reforms to a resolution of the Israeli-Palestinian conflict. Arabs understand US security guarantees for Israel, he said. "What the Arab peoples cannot fathom is why these guarantees are transformed into unrestricted backing on unrestrained Israeli policies contrary to international legality… the beast of extremism, terrorism and hatred remains with us because we are not true to our commitments. It remains to be seen whether we can for the first time be honest with each other and commit ourselves to settling the Arab-Israeli conflict."[20]

Colin Powell attempted to play down the political dimension of the reform process: at the opening session, he noted that "political and economic freedom go hand in hand… All of us confront the daily threat of terrorism. To defeat the murderous extremists in our midst, we must work together to address the causes of despair and frustration that extremists exploit for their own use."[21]

The final communiqué accepted that participants' support for reform "will go hand in hand with their support for a just, comprehensive and lasting settlement to the Arab-Israeli conflict." The communiqué made it clear that the participants would not rush into reform, and reaffirmed that it is "the sovereign right of each country…to freely develop its own democratic political and socio-cultural system," free from "interference… from outside."[22]

The participants called for specific steps to implement proposals aimed at creating greater economic development, political participation and educational opportunities in the broader Middle East and North Africa. They called for the Forum to provide "an informal, flexible, open and inclusive dialogue, devoted to strengthening democracy and the participation of civil society, to developing skills training, and to encouraging the growth of modern economies that generate wealth and that are well integrated into the global economy."[23]

Turkey, Yemen and Italy proposed the creation of a Democracy Assistance Dialogue to promote consolidation of democratic institutions in the region. The participants welcomed this initiative and affirmed their commitment to working with civil society representatives in their countries to create a solid foundation for democratic reforms. The participants also called for a stronger regional commitment to education and the elimination of illiteracy. Algeria and Afghanistan offered to sponsor a literacy workshop in Algeria in early 2005. Jordan offered to host a May 2005 meeting of the Education Ministers from the region to discuss literacy training, curricula upgrades and strategies to improve educational administration.

The participants welcomed the creation of a region-specific private enterprise development fund at the International Finance Corporation (IFC). This fund is designed to provide technical support and financial assistance to small private enterprises in the broader Middle East and North Africa region. The participants set an initial funding goal of $100 million for the IFC facility.

The government officials also endorsed the conclusions of the business dialogue group stating the need to establish higher standards of governance in the region, including greater transparency, respect for property rights, the rule of law, and effective, independent judiciaries.

The official US Government press release noted that the Forum had produced "solid initiatives". Colin Powell said that even though the initiatives discussed were not necessarily a radical departure from previously existing bilateral and multilateral programmes, the Forum for the Future "is a way of bringing it all together and coming up with a solid plan of what the needs are for each of these countries".[24] He added that, in this way, the various efforts underway and the new initiatives being undertaken could feed into a "common agenda".

In his briefing to the media, the Moroccan Communications Minister said that the Forum held in Rabat was "a non-constraining space for dialogue that concerns all Arab states and most Islamic countries."[25] He argued that change and economic and social development can only stem from the societies and peoples concerned, and cannot be imposed on any country. He added that Morocco, together with the Arab states, believed that only a comprehensive approach that takes into account all the issues posed on the Arab scene will lead to a consensus-based formula to address all these major issues, noting that "this approach also requires to pose the thorny issues, particularly the Palestinian cause and the situation in Iraq." He observed that the change and modernisation process can only emanate from inside the countries concerned as part of a comprehensive approach that addresses all the important and sensitive issues in the Arab and Islamic world. He called for "deepening dialogue" among the parties concerned, saying that dialogue is all the more necessary as the Forum is a common initiative and not a unilateral one that does take into account specificity of our countries.

On the other hand, non-official comment in the Arab world has been sharply critical both of the reluctance of the Arab leaders to initiate genuine reform in their polities as also the US approach and intentions in the region in this regard. Thus, Sati'e Noureddin wrote acerbically in the Lebanese daily, *Al-Safir*, that the meeting of the Forum was "historic" only in the sense that "it witnessed the unprecedented transformation of foreign and finance ministers from more than twenty Arab and foreign states into press commentators, who gathered together in one place to discuss issues over which they have no power to decide."[26] The Conference, according to him, had no fixed agenda, had set up no follow-up mechanism, and was without a secretariat. Noureddin concluded that the "real reform" the Americans are seeking in the Arab world is already underway: "This is reform in the fields of security cooperation, pooling intelligence, and the legal systems, none of which concerns any of the commentators taking part in the supposedly 'historical' Forum for the Future."

On similar lines, Fawaz Al-Ajami observed that everyone in the Arab world supported the reform process because "corruption, injustice, dictatorship, and the absence of popular participation are responsible for bringing the Arab world to the existing disastrous level of backwardness, disintegration, and deterioration.

And most recently, these very same factors were responsible for the US occupation that lies so heavily on the land of the Tigris and the Euphrates."[27] However, in his view, the Americans were not really interested in the establishment of a healthy and genuine democracy in the Arab world; this was because genuine democracy would lead to a rejection of US strategic schemes in this area:

> The Arab world from the [Atlantic] Ocean to the [Persian] Gulf would say 'No!' to US schemes in Iraq; 'No!' to the occupation of Iraq; 'No!' to limitless US support for the Zionist enemy and 'No!' to the US characterisation of Palestinian resistance as terrorism; 'No!' to intervention in Arab domestic affairs, 'No!' to unlimited US support for Arab dictatorial regimes, 'No!' to the US campaign against opposing points of views, such as its campaign against the Al-Jazeera satellite TV station.

Abdul Rahman Al-Nuaimi reflected similar scepticism about the intentions of the USA and the Arab regimes. He pointed out that "human rights and democracy have become tools for compromise and haggling" between the Arab states and the West.[28] He said:

> ... after every campaign of arrests in this or that Kingdom, American officials speak of the need to respect human rights. In response, they get economic, political or military concessions regarding pan-Arab or domestic issues, while the detainees remain in prison. Meanwhile, the situation remains the same, while the Americans retract their statements and our officials stress the need for deep-seated reforms that they will introduce in the near future, inshallah!

VI. The Content and Direction of Middle East Reform: Issues of Political Participation and "Islam" in the Reformed Polity

In examining the issue of reform in the Middle East, both Western and Arab commentators have set out two core issues that would constitute "reform" in the region:

(i) political participation, involving elected Parliaments and rotation of power; and,

(ii) the place of Islam in the reformed polity.

Political Participation

Both these issues have got clubbed together in the central predicament of the Arab countries which was articulated by President Hosni Mubarak to an American reporter thus: "If I were to do what you ask [i.e. provide human rights and press freedom], the fundamentalists will take over Egypt. Is that what you want?" Mubarak added: "When the Americans call for democracy, who do they think would come to power? Democrats? No. The Muslim Brotherhood would seize power in Cairo, Amman, Riyadh and Palestine."

Abdelwahab el-Effendi mentions that, in his remarks quoted above, Mubarak has unwittingly made four important admissions: *first*, he has admitted that his regime was far from democratic, contrary to what he and his National Democratic Party [NDP] have been alleging for years. Moreover, Mubarak has revealed that he has no intention whatsoever of steering his country on a path to democracy. Mubarak's *second* confession is that the Muslim Brotherhood – and not the NDP –was the most popular mass movement in Egypt today. His *third* confession is that the Muslim Brotherhood has been persecuted and oppressed for that reason, i.e. because it was so popular among Egypt's masses. The most important admission Mubarak has made, however, is that his regime has failed – despite trying for the best part of 22 years – in its efforts to subjugate the Muslim Brotherhood.[2]

The scenario presented by Mubarak has been a central American and Israeli concern in regard to "reform" in the Middle East for the last fifteen years or so, and has provided the justification for continued US support to authoritarian and repressive regimes in the Middle East. The distinguished Saudi journalist, Jamal Khashogji, has recalled in an article in *al-Watan* that, in the early 1990s, he had attended a seminar in New York, organised by the Council of Foreign Relations.[3] At the seminar, a working paper written by the journalist, Judith Miller, was circulated, which was titled: "Do Not Push for Democracy but for Human Rights in the Middle East". Khashogji affirms that, in response to the events of September 11, the US Administration has now reversed its decades-old policy of supporting repressive regimes in the Middle East and substituted it with a call for democratic reform in the region as a "means of protecting the United States against the evil resulting from despair and loss of hope" in the Middle East.

He notes that the earlier US policy in the Middle East had involved, inter alia, the deliberate reversal of the democratic process in Algeria, where democracy was replaced by a harsh military dictatorship, which resulted in a near civil war in the country involving the deaths of several thousand Algerians. Khashogji believes that the earlier US approach, as articulated by Judith Miller, was merely giving expression to a point of view that had been developed in Israel: Israel was afraid that democracy in the Arab world might bring patriotic forces to power that could rebuild their States and make them more capable of confronting its (Israel's) superiority.

It is interesting to note that the Israeli position, at least in this regard, has not changed. In a policy paper prepared by the pro-Israeli American think-tank, the Washington Institute for Near East Policy, the author, Robert Satloff, was critical about the provision in the GMEI for training of Arab Parliamentarians.[4] The reality in many Middle Eastern countries, according to him, is that "anti-American, anti-Western, anti-peace Islamists constitute large or even dominant blocs in local parliaments. An open-door policy of parliamentary training would only help such individuals become more effective critics of pro-American, pro-Western, pro-peace regional governments", an obvious reference to Israel.

Beyond Israeli self-centredness and xenophobia, and US concerns relating to the ascendancy of Islamists to power through the ballot-box, there is an abiding concern in the Arab world that true democracy is unlikely to emerge since it would have to be necessarily based on the collapse of the existing political order and its leadership; hence, it follows that existing leaderships will make every effort to ensure that such a democratic polity does not actually emerge. In this situation, the Arab people are likely to continue to be tied to an order that has outlived its relevance but is incapable of being replaced.

The pragmatic middle-path approach, which is obtaining increasing support, is for the USA to pursue a policy of slow reform over the next few years, which would set the countries concerned on the road to democracy, without immediately placing a democratic order in position. Thus, Fareed Zakaria believes that the "swamp of Islamic extremism" can be drained by making existing regimes "more legitimate in the eyes of their people."[5] The agenda set out by him is modest and, on the face of it, achievable. He sees that constitutional liberalism – made up of the rule of law, individual rights, private property, independent courts and separation of Church and State, is the ultimate aim of political reform, but recognises that it took the West hundreds of years to achieve this stage. For the Middle East, he suggests modest incremental steps in respect of different countries. Beyond this, Zakaria attaches considerable importance to economic reform: he recommends liberalising the Middle East economies so that a "genuine entrepreneurial class" emerges as a force for change in the region. He also suggests that Islamic groups should be increasingly permitted to enter the electoral process so that their involvement in day-to-day politics and assumption of political responsibility will dilute their extremist fervour, while simultaneously removing the aura they may have on account of their links with the divine!

The premier American neocon visionary, Paul Wolfowitz, seems to accept the need for such a modest political agenda for the Middle East. In an interview in December 2002, Wolfowitz said:

> How many places besides England and the US really are Jeffersonian democracies? There are a few. But there are an awful lot of imperfect democracies that are just huge strides ahead of where they were 10 or 20 years ago.[6]

He then added:

> Democracy is certainly about more than one man, one vote, one time. That's why free markets are so important. That's why the institutions of civil society have come to be recognised increasingly as important. And those kinds of things – institutional foundations of democracy and liberty – require an institutional setting that has to grow. We can't create them ourselves. We certainly can't impose them on people who don't want them or don't have the commitment or energy or education levels.[7]

It appears that for the present at least radical political transformation is not on the American or Arab agenda.

Islam

The place of Islam in the reformed Arab polity is a more complex subject. Several commentators have observed that any reform of the polity, for it to be acceptable to the populace, must be sensitive to the place of Islam in Arab society. Ahmed Abbas Saleh argues that religious ideology is "an integral component of local culture in the Middle East," and Islam "has always constituted the cultural and ideological foundation on which various governments in the region have been based. Though there were several reform movements in different Muslim countries throughout its history, no movement called for abandoning Islam." He points out that, even Mohammed Ali (1769-1849), who vigorously sought to modernise Egypt with the help of foreign advisors, did not abandon the country's Islamic character.[8]

The predicament the average Muslim faces today in regard to reconciling modernism on Western lines with his traditional religious beliefs is not unique: it is in line with the dilemmas faced by his co-religionists in previous decades and centuries as well as by Christian and other religious communities at different periods of their political evolution. Indeed, it remains a central issue of debate in Western societies even today.

Islamic societies have at no time been static: it is important to recall that the essential feature of Islamic societies through the ages has been dialogue – dialogue between tradition and innovation, between the past and the contemporary, between the peaceful and the violent, between the intellectual and the pedant, between the obscurantist and the modern. It is on the basis of these dialogues and negotiations that Muslims attempted to cope with the changing environment and the fresh challenges posed by new socio-economic and political developments, both internal and external. The Saudi intellectual, Yusif Makki, notes that, in modern Arab history, there have been regular calls for reform from intellectuals steeped in Islamic ethos and culture, who demanded an end to discrimination between Muslim sects, liberating the mind from superstition, and, above all, an end to tyranny, which they saw as the root of all evil.[8a] Similarly, Usama Ghazali Harb affirms that "calls for reform and development in the Islamic world have been at the top of the agenda of many enlightened intellectuals – Arabs and Muslims, for more than a century and a half, a long time before US and Western politicians and intellectuals discovered them."[9]

However, Arab commentators, as also Western academics, recommend considerable caution in attempting to transplant modern, Western models onto Arab societies. Thus, the Saudi sociologist, Madhawi al-Rashid, has advised Saudi reformers to avoid making extravagant demands for constitutional monarchy, and has suggested, instead, that they come up with a vision based on the Arab-Muslim nature of Saudi society. She has urged them to "refrain from using slogans that most Saudis cannot identify with."[10]

In light of the US approach to the development of a new political order in Iraq, as also the comments made by some American academics in the context of the Middle East reform initiative, certain Arab intellectuals have expressed concern that the US-led initiative would exclude any compromise with the region's Islamic ethos. In this context, Marwan Al-Kabalan has recalled the assertion by the US Administrator in Iraq, Paul Bremer, who said, "the law in Iraq must be based on secular principles." Kabalan maintains that such an approach not only violates the notion of democracy, which implies electing a government that reflects the free will of the people, it also shows "arrogance and ignorance about the region and its culture." Kabalan went on to say:

> US officials are still unable to understand that Islam is the religion and culture of the entire Arab world and that it is part and parcel of the local traditions, customs and laws and, hence, it cannot be removed merely because the US does not like Islam, Muslims or Islamists.
>
> Any plan intended to minimise the role of Islam in Arab politics and society is doomed to failure.[11]

In the discourse relating to the contemporary Islamic world in general and particularly the question of reform, there has been a tendency on the part of Western rightwing intellectuals to speak of "Islam" in generalised, essentialised terms and to see Muslim people as "the Other". In this exercise, certain broad-brush characteristics are readily attributed to the community, with little regard to geography, historical experience or contemporary political/cultural setup. Though occasionally caveats are added to suggest variety and complexity, a monolithic approach remains pervasive and is ultimately the most influential.

The "clash-of-civilisations" academics such as Bernard Lewis and Samuel Huntington have been the most important in the promotion of this view, with significant contributions from pro-Israeli rightwing polemicists such as Daniel Pipes and many others. The problem is more acute when it comes to non-specialist commentators, who in newspapers, monographs and seminar papers, vigorously present an ideology-driven point of view and approach, influenced primarily by the neocon mindset in regard to understanding and coming to terms with the Arab/Islamic world and the way it grapples with the issue of reform.

In this context, an examination of a recent monograph by Cheryl Benard titled: "Civil Democratic Islam: Partners, Resources and Strategies", published by the National Security Research Division of RAND Corporation, is particularly instructive.[12] The mindset of the author in regarding "Islam" as "the Other" is revealed in the first paragraph of the summary itself, where the author states:

> There is no question that contemporary Islam is in a volatile state, engaged in an internal and external struggle over its values, its identity, and its place in the world. Rival versions are contending for spiritual and political dominance. This conflict has serious costs and economic, social, political, and security implications for the rest of the world. Consequently, the West is making an increased effort to come to terms with, to understand, and to influence the outcome of this struggle.
>
> Islam's current crisis has two main components: a failure to thrive and loss of connection to the global mainstream. The Islamic world has been marked by a long period of backwardness and comparative powerlessness; many different solutions, such as nationalism, pan-Arabism, Arab socialism, and

Islamic revolution, have been attempted without success, and this has led to frustration and anger. At the same time, the Islamic world has fallen out of step with contemporary global culture, an uncomfortable situation for both sides.[13]

Having thus succinctly set out her view on the state of affairs of "contemporary Islam", Benard then presents the American wish-list in the most patronising terms:

> Clearly, the United States, the modern industrialised world, and indeed the international community as a whole would prefer an Islamic world that is compatible with the rest of the system: democratic, economically viable, politically stable, socially progressive, and follows the rules and norms of international conduct. They also want to prevent a "clash of civilisations" in all of its possible variants—from increased domestic unrest caused by conflicts between Muslim minorities and "native" populations in the West to increased militancy across the Muslim world and its consequences, instability and terrorism.[14]

In pursuit of her agenda, in simplistic "we-they" terms, Benard divides all Muslims into four categories:[15]

(i) *Fundamentalist*: those who reject democratic values and contemporary Western culture;

(ii) *Traditionalist*, who are conservative and suspicious of modernity, innovation and change;

(iii) *Modernist*, who wish to modernise and reform Islam and to bring it into line with the contemporary times; and,

(iv) *Secularist,* who believe in separation of church and State, with religion being relegated to the private sphere.

Benard's game-plan in dealing with "Islam" is clear:[16]

(i) support the modernist first;

(ii) support the traditionalist against the fundamentalist;

(iii) confront and oppose the fundamentalist;

(iv) selectively support the secularist.

To her credit, Benard recognises certain problems in implementing her game-plan. She is aware that " the secularist should be our most natural ally in the Muslim world," but notes with regret that many important secularists in the Islamic world are "unfriendly or even extremely hostile to us on other grounds."[17] Benard also notes that certain authors "believe that fundamentalist hostility to the United States and to the West primarily reflects anger over some aspects of our foreign policy or discomfort over the more liberal aspects of Western culture." While conceding that this could be true to some extent, Benard quickly makes the general assertion that "fundamentalism represents a basic and total rejection of democracy and all the core values of modern civil society."[18]

While it is not necessary to provide here a detailed critique of Cheryl Benard's tract,[19] it suffices to note that it is a clear and succinct representation of the neocon approach to the Islamic world, epitomised by the central divide between "Islam" and the "West", where the West, particularly the United States, represents the values of "global modernity". These values, according to Benard, are under attack from an assertive Islam, to which she believes the United States must respond by "affirming the values of Western civilisations".[20] In Benard's world-view, as in that of others of her ilk, regions of considerable geographical, historical and cultural breadth and complexity can be conveniently categorised into monolithic compartments. In such a discourse there is no suggestion of variety and no indication that even basic concepts such as those of personal and national identity, national and civilisational values, and cultural and religious norms, are not cast in stone either in "Islam" or the "West", but are contested territory, and subject to constant debate, review and re-definition.

Moving away from Benard's self-righteous stridency, we find a more sober and cautious approach in the paper "Secularism and Democracy in the Middle East" by Elizabeth Shakman Hurd.[21] Hurd argues that the central challenge facing the countries of the Middle East in the 21st century is "developing a legitimate practice of democracy that avoids the pitfalls of both authoritarian secularism and militant Islamism." According to her, the successful facing of this challenge requires that secularism, as accepted by certain existing

Arab regimes, [such as in Egypt, Syria and Saddam's Iraq], be suitably modified if it is to become a legitimate alternative to militant Islam. She asserts that in the contemporary Middle East, secularism has been appropriated as the legitimising principle for the suppression of indigenous political thought and practice. It has contributed to "the attempt to 'take possession' of the Middle East in the name of a modern, Western democratic ideal." In the Middle East, Hurd maintains, secularism has been associated with opposition to Islam and indiscriminate support for Western power. Middle East ruling classes have appropriated secularism as an instrument for legitimising their repressive actions in the region.

According to Hurd, secularism, by excluding the religious element, has in fact compromised democratic politics, and has led to the radicalisation of Islamic political parties and even to terrorism against Western targets. Hence, she believes, it is necessary for the international community to encourage "pluralistic democracy even if it means supporting religious parties".

Hurd concludes that there is a need to arrange a compromise between the secular *v/s* theological divide. Towards this end, in her view, secularism must engage with and incorporate local traditions of governance, specifically accommodating alternative concepts and practices of religion, politics, ethics and democracy. She notes that secularism in the Middle East has tended to equate Muslim religious belief with political dogma, and its manifestation in the public sphere with political dogmatism or fanaticism. The sensible approach, according to her, is that public religiosity be accepted in the public sphere "as long as it is accompanied by respect for competing perspectives." This process of compromise, according to Hurd, will lend "legitimacy to the efforts of those who seek to elaborate a pluralistic, neo-Islamist, neo-secular model of democracy in the region."

Amy Hawthorne, participating in a round-table discussion on Arab reform in October 2003, raised the basic question as to whether democracy in the Arab world would actually lead to "secularisation" which she believed was "at the heart of the Bush Administration's transformative vision for the region".[22] She pointed out that fundamental political change does not necessarily or inevitably lead to the establishment of democracy and, in this context, raised doubts about the US-led political processes underway in Iraq. According to Hawthorne, democratisation in the Arab world would involve the shaping of new national identities which would take place in response to how the United States is perceived. In this process, according to her, religion in its various forms and interpretations would perhaps be "the most effective and authentic vehicle to shape the indigenous and authentic local identity." Flowing from this, Hawthorne concluded that even as democratisation takes place in the Arab world, "we should be prepared to expect the rise [in] the influence of religious values and ideas in shaping governance."

This acceptance of the presence of Islam in the

reformed polity is not just confined to academics. It is interesting to note that, unlike the Jewish neocons who see "Islam" as the generalised "Other," their *Christian fundamentalist* allies occasionally indicate a different view of Islam and Muslim societies. Thus, the Christian fundamentalist leader, Amitai Etzioni, who is the founder of the Christian Communitarian Movement [said to enjoy considerable influence in the Bush White House], has spoken approvingly of the goal of the reformers in Iran to establish a "religious civil society". He points out:

> The fact that to Western ears a "religious civil society" sounds like an oxymoron is precisely what is wrong with Western thinking.
>
> The West should not export the French or American idea of separation of religion and state, but instead draw in moderate mullahs and other religious figures as one of the best ways to shore up social order...
>
> Instead of being replaced with secular schools, religious schools should be allowed to exist as long as they provide education in subjects such as science and math, their teachers are qualified by educational authorities, and their religious texts reflect moderate rather than virulent Islam.[23]

He recommends strongly that the reform constitutions in Islamic countries should not entail coercive secularisation, as Turkey's first President, Mustafa Kemal Ataturk, imposed, but make room for moderate Islamic tenets.[24]

"Moderate" Islam

Overwhelmed and appalled at the carnage

wrought by vengeful and merciless extremists, the Islamic establishment and political leaders across the Muslim world are today forcefully articulating the discourse of moderation, tolerance and dialogue, accompanied by the severest criticism of Islamic radicals committing murder in the name of religion. Thus, in his Friday sermon, in April 2004, Sheikh Saleh bin Abdullah bin Humaid, the Imam of the Haram Sharif, Makkah, said:

> ...extremism in Allah's religion is a cause for destruction and sedition. They [the extremists] are fanatic regarding the religious scholars they follow and consider some Muslims and their rulers as disbelievers. They isolate themselves from the Muslim society and confuse between ignorance and being unjust to the people. The fate of the extremists is destruction. The methods of extremists through use of violence, carrying out explosions, destruction, robbery and shedding blood, will defeat neither the great values nor will they undermine the great accomplishments. They cannot liberate a people or impose a sect on people.
>
> Terrorism and bloodshed cannot be a respectable system or an acceptable course. Nor can it be a creed or religion. They cannot change any policy and will not win sympathy. They confirm an aggressive nature and a bloody spirit. Therefore, sensible people appreciate this united stance by the *Ummah* against these blatant criminal acts.[25]

The Saudi Islamic writer, Abdul Rahman Al-Rashi, saw extremism as the curse of Islam from its inception; he recommended:

> Islam's enemy has always been, first and foremost,

> extremism. The people who should fight them are preachers themselves. It is their duty to publicise middle-of-the road Islam and back moderate preachers....Since these people [extremists] tried to use Muslim funds under the pretext of a *jihad* that killed more Muslims than members of any other group, it is the duty of charities to turn around and back the awareness campaigns against extremism....*It is time to rescue Islam from the Islamists and save its reputation.* (Emphasis added.)[26]

Another Saudi scholar bemoaned the wave of violence in his country and explained it thus:[27]

> This wave of violence that has swept across Saudi Arabia does not surprise me. The sermons and behaviour that have been a constant feature in our society were bound to lead to this, if not more. How can you expect to convince a 30-year-old fanatic that what he is doing is wrong, unethical and pure madness when for the past 20 years of his existence he has been the subject of a long, highly intensive extremism course?
>
> Teaching children from when they begin to interact with the world for over 12 years about Islam in that is confrontational and rigid only serves to fuel the fires of hatred. Further inflammation through the Friday prayers and evening sermons then whips up a fire so big that it will consume a huge area before it can be put out – just as we are seeing now.
>
> It is painfully ironic, when looking back into the annals of Arab culture, to see how Arabs prided themselves and were known for their honour, generosity and hospitality. Now we are known for a completely different set of qualities, and our honour has been ground into the dust. Unless we all stand up and overturn the extremist hold on our country,

then we can only expect more bloodshed.

King Fahd of Saudi Arabia, in his speech at the opening session of the Shoura Council, described terrorism as "corruption on earth."[28] Noting that Muslims were responsible for some terrorist acts, he said that Islam had nothing to do with such conduct and action. According to him:

> Islam is free of such acts and the Muslim has nothing to do with these actions and has no sympathy for those who carry them out. Islam is the religion of peace, love and tolerance. It calls for doing good and refraining from anything evil and encourages understanding and peaceful coexistence while strongly warning against injustice and aggression.

With the exception of the neocons and their intellectual and political allies, the emerging consensual view in the Middle East and the West is that, while "Islam" will constitute the cultural core of the reformed polity, its principal attributes will be those of tolerance and accommodation, with an emphasis on inter-sectarian and inter-civilisational dialogue and understanding. At the same time, observers of the Islamic scene accept that present-day conditions are not propitious for the encouragement of a moderate discourse in contemporary Islam. The ongoing US-led war on terror, which appears to primarily target Muslim countries and peoples, has fomented a strong wave of anti-Americanism across the Arab and Islamic world, together with increasing estrangement of the people from their regimes, which, in the words of Graham Fuller, are seen "led by supine dictators, who depend on harsh security services to stay in power, who are powerless to change realities in the Arab world, who cling to tight relations with Washington at any cost to preserve their power."[29]

However, even in this uncongenial environment, Fuller sees some positive signs. These emerge, ironically enough, from the increasing participation of various Islamic parties in the politics of their countries. This competition among Islamic groups different espousing beliefs and approaches has meant that no single group can claim the monopoly of religious sanction for its political beliefs and actions.

Again, participation in domestic politics has in itself fostered an increasing review of radical postures and actions and has encouraged a propensity to accommodation and moderation. This has been further buttressed by the fact that active involvement with national politics has meant greater exposure to the realities of the country's social and economic problems and the constraints upon political leaders in addressing them, all of which enhance the value of pragmatism.

VII. Overview and Prognosis

The interest of the US to promote freedom and democracy in the Middle East, fiercely articulated for the last three years by President Bush and his senior officials, marks a significant departure from consistent US policy in the Middle East of the last 50 years or so. During this period, the US had believed that its interests in the region—competition with communism; security of oil resources, and security of Israel—were best served by policies that ensured stability in the region even if this was achieved by authoritarian dictatorships or repressive traditional monarchies. Through the 1990s, the US policy in the region did not undergo any significant change: the confrontation with Communism was merely replaced by confrontation with Islamic extremism. Accordingly, the policy of tolerating autocracy, repression and rampant abuse of human rights continued.

The events of September 11 dramatically conveyed to the US leadership how short-sighted and misguided its policies had been: it now saw that the very countries that had been its closest allies had in fact nurtured its worst enemies. The US leaders were convinced that this swamp of Islamic extremism had been nourished by autocracy and repression, which had engendered extraordinary rage against the ruling regimes and, by extension, the US that sustained them in power. American analysts also concluded that, given the absence of legitimate outlets for expression of dissent, such domestic anger would primarily be expressed through "Islam": each of the Middle East countries had within it Islamic groups and movements, several of them enjoying state patronage, which nursed the dissent and rage, and provided the impulse and opportunity to express it, including through terrorist violence.

Since September 11, President Bush has been harping on this theme. Most recently, in his inaugural address on January 20, 2005, he said: "For as long as whole regions of the world simmer in resentment and tyranny – prone to ideologies that feed hatred and excuse murder – violence will gather, and multiply in destructive power, and cross the most defended borders, and raise a mortal threat."[1] He asserted that relations with the United States would be conditioned by the way in which governments treated their own people. Later, in his "State of the Union" address on February 2, 2005, Bush was both specific in his reference to the Middle East and categorical in demanding political change. He repeated his earlier point that regions mired in despair and hatred are "the recruiting grounds for terror". He then went on to assert: "America will stand with the allies of freedom to support democratic movements in the Middle East and beyond, with the ultimate goal of ending tyranny in our world."[2]

Developments in the Middle East in the first three months of 2005 have led President Bush and sections of the Western media to trumpet the "success" of the Bush Doctrine in promoting democracy in the region.

The specific references in this regard are to the general election in Iraq; the Presidential election in Palestine following the death of Yasser Arafat; the massive demonstrations in Lebanon seeking the withdrawal of Syrian forces and a democratic order; the statement of President Hosni Mubarak of Egypt allowing the opposition to put up candidates against him when he stands for re-election; and, finally, the municipal elections in Saudi Arabia from February 2005.[3] The *Economist* caught the spirit of this triumphalism when it said:

> However much Arabs resent America's intervention in Iraq – and most still do – the election there, a month ago, has plainly struck a chord across the region. Without a doubt, something exciting is in the air. Democracy for Arabs can no longer be dismissed as the stuff of foolish dreamers.[4]

However, even the *Economist* conceded the need for caution; it noted that "the Middle East is still a dangerous mess", and things could go badly wrong, particularly in regard to Iraq and the Middle East peace process. *The Sunday Times* of London has spoken of "the Arabian spring", with the Arab region "potentially on the verge of changes of tectonic proportions."[5] But, it accepts that, while there is a clear trend in favour of change, there is no clarity about the impulse behind it nor certainty about the future.

There is every reason to be cautious and to eschew euphoria and triumphalism. The contemporary political scenario in the region is made up of three elements which have important implications for the reform process: the continuing US military occupation of Iraq, with armed resistance from various sections of the Iraqi population and persistent revelations of gross abuses by US and other coalition forces on Iraqi civilians; unabated Israeli violence against the Palestinians, accompanied by sporadic acts of terror from the Palestinian side; and recurring acts of terrorist violence in different parts of the globe but particularly in the Islamic world, by individuals and groups affiliated to the Al Qaeda ideology. These factors continue to engender estrangement between the Arab and Islamic people on the one hand and the "West", led by the US, on the other, setting the stage for a possible long-drawn and violent "clash of civilisations."

The US continues to have little moral authority and less credibility as a sponsor of reform and change due to its record in the region and the widespread perception that its strategic interests have a continued need for and even dependence on authoritarian regimes which would sub-serve its interests particularly in regard to energy, Israel, and combating extremist Islam. Such an environment scarcely appears propitious for the promotion of economic and cultural reform and political change.

Is it then possible to be optimistic about reform in the Arab world? It cannot be denied that, in spite of the apparently unfavourable environment for reform and the low credibility of its sponsor, the idea of reform and change has gripped the imagination and spirit of the region's populace, sweeping in its wake intellectuals, businessmen, educationists, economists, civil servants, members of civil society, religious personages, and even political leaders. Indeed, it has come to occupy central space in contemporary Middle East political discourse. Hundreds of newspaper editorials and *op-ed* pieces across the Arab world have examined reform from different angles, all of them expressing the considered view of the region that rejects the status quo and seeks, even demands, change. Differences exist in regard to detail, emphasis and timing, but there is a resounding consensus on the urgent need for political, economic and cultural reform.

Demand for reform has also been presented through government-sponsored conferences attended by NGOs and intellectuals which have taken place since early 2004 in different cities of the Arab world, such as Sana'a, Doha, Amman and Alexandria. The "Declarations" emerging from these conferences, with government supervision and approval, have articulated the same message: calls for popular participation in the political process, enforcement of the rule of law, respect for human rights, and empowerment of women.

Hardly any Arab country has remained untouched. Saudi Arabia, the bastion of Islamic/Wahhabi conservatism, has witnessed, over the last few months, an upsurge of extremist violence accompanied by strident demands for change in all spheres of national life, through newspaper editorials, petitions submitted to the rulers, and public conferences sponsored by the government. In September 2003, a new petition, signed by 300 intellectuals, including 50 women, was submitted to Crown Prince Abdullah. This petition called for radical reforms in the country's constitutional, political, economic and social institutions.[6]

Between December 27-31, 2003, the "Second National Dialogue Forum", was held, in Makkah. Attended by 60 clergymen, intellectuals and academics, both men and women, and 10 specialist researchers, its theme was : "Excess and Moderation : A Thorough Review." The Forum made, *inter alia,* the following recommendations:[7]

i) need to accelerate the political reform process, including elections to the Shoura Council, and setting up of trade unions and civil society institutions;

ii) financial transparency and accountability;

iii) modernising the religious message;

iv) promoting dialogue in Saudi society and "responsible free speech";

v) reforming education to spread the spirit of tolerance and moderation;

vi) strengthening the role of women in all aspects of life; and

vii) guaranteeing a fair trial to those accused of violence and terrorism.

In March 2004, the Kingdom set up a National Human Rights Commission, which had been preceded, in November 2003, by the first human rights conference in Riyadh.[8] Again, in mid-June, 2004, the third National

Dialogue Forum met in Jeddah, this time focusing on the "Rights and Duties of Women." The Forum reconfirmed that "women could be their own guardian," and recommended expansion of educational and employment opportunities for them.[9] Finally, since February 2005, Saudi Arabia has witnessed municipal elections, commencing with elections for the Riyadh municipal council on February 10, 2005, with subsequent rounds scheduled to take place in different parts of the country upto April 2005. The fact that the franchise was restricted to men evoked considerable criticism from prominent Saudi women (and several men as well). Now, there are demands that women be nominated to the Shoura Council.

While at first sight the process of reform in Saudi Arabia appears hesitant and halting, the fact remains that, for the first time in recent Saudi history, issues of political participation, moderation in religious discourse, transparency and accountability in the economic arena, the status of women, and inter-denominational and inter-religious dialogue, are being aired in public, with liberal intellectuals debating these issues vigorously with government officials and the Wahhabi clergy.

Across the Arab world, people have increasingly come to the streets to condemn US policies and to make demands for political reform. Demonstrations have reportedly taken place in Saudi Arabia, Oman, Bahrain, Egypt and in Lebanon, indicating a possible erosion of the fear of the State and its security apparatus. Newspapers in the region have been robust in criticising the Arab polities and the policies of their leaders, and demanding early remedial action. In this environment, Arab political leaders, confused and reluctant though they may be, have had no choice but to take cognisance of the deteriorating strategic environment and the fervent calls for change from their people. In March 2004, they were divided and dithering and unable to develop a consensual response to the challenge of change presented specifically by the publication of the US-sponsored Greater Middle East Initiative the previous month. However, within a few weeks, this hesitation came to an end, and the Arab summiteers approved, in May 2004, the "Tunis Declaration" that commits them to embrace reform.

The OIC too has recognised the reform spirit pervading the Islamic world. Pakistan sponsored an international symposium on "enlightened moderation" (June 1-2, 2004), at which the then OIC Secretary General called on Islamic countries "to oppose religious extremism, fanaticism and bigotry", and "disseminate in our societies the culture of tolerance". He also called on Muslims to inculcate the "modern political and social values" which include good governance, rule of law, political participation and pluralism, as also the principles of transparency and accountability.[10]

The OIC Secretary General continued to speak on these lines at the inaugural session of the Istanbul ICFM (June 14-16, 2004). Early in his address, the Secretary General said: "it is evidently high time to take a decisive position on democracy."[11] He went on to say :

> "We can work such a renewal of our systems of government that guarantees the peaceful, legitimate alternation of power, while ensuring the respect of public rights, justice, equality, as well as intellectual and cultural openness. Then and only then can we become part of the fabric of the worldwide moderate movement."

The Secretary General also noted with regret the parlous state of Islamic education and culture and the marginalisation of women.

However, in spite of the prevailing ferment, enthusiasm and consensus in support of reform, it is natural for an observer in the region to be sceptical, even cynical. Recent Middle East history is replete with promises of change based on the peace process, road maps, conferences, declarations, agreements, and solemn rhetoric, all of which have dashed against the rock of US's strategic interests and the self-centredness and venality of its Arab allies. Hence, some commentators, American, European and Arab, believe that this present-day ferment and enthusiasm too shall dissipate in face of US political compulsions, the short-sightedness of Arab leaders, and, above all, the unfertile soil for reform that prevails in the region, particularly the absence of the ethos and institutions that would engender freedom and democracy.

The sense of pessimism is strengthened by the deteriorating security environment. Arab leaders have frequently justified delaying political reform on the ground that the Arab world is in a state of war with Israel and, in general, faces extraordinary external and internal challenges, which taken together provide a non-conducive climate for reform. There is no doubt that US military action in Iraq, its continued occupation of that country, and its avowed commitment to intrusive policies and hegemonic approach have imbued the already volatile region with a deep sense of insecurity and apprehension. Objective American commentators agree that democracy-building in the Arab world would be strengthened with a more even-handed US approach to the Palestinian question, which would include active US opposition to the extremist policies of the Likud in Israel and a just settlement of the Palestinian question, together with the exit of the US forces from Iraq and the region and, in general, a more accommodative and sympathetic US approach to Islam and Muslims.

While it may suit the Bush administration and the right-wing US/UK media to take credit for the winds of change in the Arab world, the factual position is that this urge for reform had already been making itself felt before 9/11; indeed, the case can be made that, but for US neocon-driven policies, resort to armed action in Iraq, continued military occupation of Iraq, and confrontationist policies *vis-à-vis* Syria and Iran, the pace of reform would have been faster and some real change achieved by now. Contrary to what the neocons may believe, the Iraqis who participated in the elections in January 2005 did so not because they had any faith in the US's democratic credentials but because they thought this would expedite the end of US occupation of their country.

At the same time, it is also likely that the US/UK

media campaign highlighting the significance of the Iraq elections in encouraging reform in the region is primarily aimed at persuading Western populations about the efficacy of US policies in the Middle East to shore up dwindling European support while balancing the continuing bad news from Iraq pertaining to sustained resistance to US occupation, mounting casualties among US personnel and in the Iraqi population (details of which are shrouded in secrecy due to restrictions on information flows), and tales of abuse of prisoners and ordinary Iraqi civilians, all of which have made the American image uglier and its position in favour of reform less credible.

Still, though the political environment in the region appears to be unpropitious for change, the rationale and momentum for reform remain: the status quo is not tenable and, regardless of the wishes of the Americans and their autocratic Arab allies, the demand for political and social reform will have to be satisfactorily addressed. There are several reasons for this.

First, beyond the unpredictable implications of the deteriorating situation in Iraq and Palestine, the robust and intrusive US military posture in the region, and the pusillanimous posture of Arab regimes, a number of domestic factors such as the burgeoning population, economic stagnation, unemployment of youth, corruption, and, above all, the violence of extremist Islam, all of these have alienated Arab populations from their governments and fostered strong popular resentments. A quick perusal of the two AHDRs is sufficient to show how serious are the socio-economic and cultural problems in the region which need to be addressed urgently. More important is the fact that Arab populations are much better educated and informed than ever before due to satellite television and the internet, and have greater awareness of the serious economic malaise in their region, and global campaigns in support of human rights, transparency and accountability, and the rights of women.

The second factor favouring reform is that the proposed reform does not contest or reject the Islamic ethos of the region. There had been concerns earlier that, in the American perspective, the September 11 attacks illustrated the need to eradicate all manifestations of political Islam, from Al Qaeda to the Muslim Brotherhood. This extreme view is now not advocated by most commentators other than extreme right-wing elements driven by pro-Israeli fervour and the "clash-of-civilisations" thesis. The general view is that continuing to "exclude or marginalise Islamist political participation would doom democracy by silencing a voice that resonates with an important segment of the public."[12] It is accepted that Islamic organisations, the bulk of which are moderate, have substantial social reform programmes, and enjoy a high standing among the populace, should be distinguished from their extremist and violent counterparts, and enabled to participate in the proposals for change in the region, particularly in the political process.

Finally, a quick and radical transformation of Arab polities is not being sought either by the bulk of the population and their rulers or even by Western governments. Reform packages proposed for the short and even the medium-term are modest and take into account the valid concern that present-day Arab leaderships would resist a rapid movement towards democracy and constitutional monarchy which would ultimately end their rule. The most likely (though not inevitable) scenario for reform is that existing regimes will lead the process by focusing on economic reform and "good governance" issues such as providing freer debates on political, social and religious reform; bringing about an improvement in the human rights situation; effecting economic reform through greater transparency in the area of government revenues and expenditures; implementing legal and judicial reform; providing an increased modicum of freedom of speech and association, organising indirect and, in due course, direct elections, and, above all, expanding the powers of the hitherto nominated and supine legislatures which would increasingly become elected bodies.

It has to be accepted that neither the Arab region nor the Americans are yet ready for radical transformation. As the *Economist* itself has frankly noted: "...the Americans know it is risky to promote ideas that threaten the regimes of some of their closest yet far from democratic allies in the wider region, such as Pakistan, Egypt, Jordan and Saudi Arabia."[13] There can be little doubt that in the area of reform, political interests will triumph over democratic ideals.

The Arab world is today at a cross-road: there is a powerful urge for across-the-board change in the polity which confronts an entrenched and reluctant leadership and its external ally, the USA, that speaks the language of reform and democracy, but whose actions–occupation, violence and abuse in the region and an enduring alliance with the potentates–raise serious doubts about the value of its utterances and the genuineness of its commitment to reform. The popular mood in the region swings from optimism when some demands for reform are conceded (e.g. municipal elections in Saudi Arabia) to cynicism, pessimism and despair when faced with the unchecked abuse of the powerful external player, the unabated violence of Israel, and the weakness and cowardice of leaders who fail to provide the inspirational leadership and dignity their people yearn for.

At this point, the situation could move in either direction: if the USA shows statesmanship in Iraq and Palestine and the Arab leaders exhibit wisdom and a long-term vision, much good could emerge; but, the record of both so far is poor and unpromising in this regard. This would have to change, and change radically, if the Arab world is to see reform.

APPENDIX I

The Greater Middle East Partnership Initiative

The following is the text of a US working paper for G-8 Sherpas, in preparation for the next G-8 Summit, at Sea Island, Georgia in the US on June 8-10. While it defines the Middle East as "the countries of the Arab world Plus Pakistan, Afghanistan, Iran, Turkey and Israel", the paper makes no reference to the last five states. Nor does it make reference to the political background of the Middle East or the Arab - Israeli conflict. An Arabic translation of the paper was published by al-Hayat *on February 13.*

The Greater Middle East (GME) region poses a unique challenge and opportunity for the international community. The three "deficits" identified by the Arab authors of the 2002 and 2003 UN Arab Human Development Reports (AHDR)—Freedom, knowledge, and women's empowerment—have contributed to conditions that threaten the national interests of all G-8 members. So long as the region's pool of politically and economically disenfranchised individuals grows, we will witness an increase in extremism, terrorism, international crime, and illegal migration. The statistics describing the current situation in the GME are daunting.

- The combined GDP of the 22 Arab League countries is less than that of Spain.
- Approximately 40 per cent of Adult Arab — 65mn

people — are illiterate, two thirds of whom are women.

- Over 50mn young people will enter the labour market by 2010, and 100mn will enter by 2020 - a minimum of 6mn new jobs need to be created each year to absorb these new entrants.

- If current unemployment rates persist, regional unemployment will reach 25mn by 2010.

- One third of the region lives on less that $2 a day. To improve standards of living, economic growth in the region must more than double from below 3 per cent currently to at least 6 per cent.

- Only 1.6 per cent of the population has access to the internet, a figure lower than that in other regions of the world, including sub-Saharan Africa.

- Women occupy just 3.5 per cent of parliamentary seats in Arab countries, compared with, for example, 8.4 per cent in sub-Saharan Africa.

- 51 per cent of older Arab youths expressed a desire to emigrate to other countries, according to the 2002 AHDR, with Europeans countries the favourite destination.

These statistics reflect a region that stands at a crossroad. The GME continue on the same path, adding every year to its population of underemployed, undereducated, and politically disenfranchised youths.

Doing so will pose a direct threat to the stability of the region, and to the common interests of the G-8 members.

The alternative is the route to reform. The two Arab Human Development Reports represent compelling and urgent calls for action in the GME. These calls have been echoed by activists, academics, and the private sector throughout the region. Some GME leaders have already heeded these calls and have steps towards political, social, and economic reforms. The Euro-Mediterranean Partnership, the US Middle East Partnership Initiative, and the multilateral reconstruction efforts in Afghanistan and Iraq demonstrate the G-8's commitment to reform in the region.

---

1. The "Greater Middle East" refers to the countries of the Arab world, plus Pakistan, Afghanistan, Iran, Turkey and Israel.

The demographic change described above, the liberation of Afghanistan and Iraq from oppressive regimes, and the emergence of democratic impluses across the region, together present the G-8 with a historic opportunity. At Sea Island, the G-8 should forge a long-term partnership with the Greater Middle East's reform leaders and launch a coordinated response to promote political, economic and social reforms in the region. The G-8 could agree on common reforms priorities that would address the AHDR deficits by.

- Promoting democracy and good governance ;
- Building a knowledge society; and
- Expanding economics opportunities.

These reform priorities are the key to the region's developments: democracy and good governance form the framework within which development takes place, well-educated individuals are the agents of development, and enterprise is the engine of development.

1. Promoting Democracy and Good Governance

"There is a substantial lag between Arab countries and other regions in terms of participatory governance... This freedom deficit undermines human development and is one of the most painful manifestations of lagging political development."

Arab Human Development Report, 2002

Democracy and freedom are essential to the flourishing of individual initiative, but are solely lacking throughout the GME. In Freedom House's 2003 report, Israel was the only GME country rated "free" and just four others were defined as "partly free". The AHDR noted that out of seven world regions, the Arab countries had the lowest in the world. Further, the Arab world rank above only sub-Saharan Africa in the empowerment of women. These discouraging indicators hardly square with the expressed wishes of the region's people : in the 2003 AHDR, for example, Arab topped the worldwide list of those supporting the statement that "democracy is better than any other form of government, and expressed the highest level of rejection of authoritarian rule.

The G-8 could show its support for democratic

reform in the region by committing to:

Free Elections Initiative: Between 2004 and 2006, numerous GME countries[2] have announced intentions to hold presidential, parliamentary, or municipal elections. Working with those countries that demonstrate a serious willingness to hold free and fair elections, the G-8 could actively provide pre-election assistance by:

- Providing technical assistance, through exchange or seminars, to establish or strengthen independent election commissions to monitor elections, respond to complains and receive reports.
- Providing technical assistance for voter registration and civic education to requesting governments, with a particular emphasis on women voters.

Parliamentary Exchange and Training: In order to strengthen the role of parliaments in democratising countries, the G-8 could sponsor exchange of parliamentarians, with a focus on drafting legislation, implementing legislative and legal reform, and representing constituents.

Women's Leadership: Academies: Women occupy just 3.5 per cent of parliaments seats in Arab countries. In order to increase women's participation in political and civic life, the G-8 could sponsor women's training academies to provide leadership training for elective office or establishing/operative an NGO. The academies could bring together female leaders from G-8 countries and the region.

2. Afghanistan, Algeria, Bahrain, Iran, Lebanon, Morocco, Qatar, Saudi Arabia, Tunisia, Turkey, and Yemen have elections scheduled.

Grassroots Legal Aid: While the US, the EU, the UN and the World Bank have already undertaken numerous initiative to promote legal and judicial reform, most are working at the national level in areas such as judicial training, judicial administration and legal code reform. AG-8 initiative could complement these efforts by focusing at the grassroots community level, where the true perception of justices begins. The G-8 could establish and fund centres at which individuals can access legal advice on civil, criminal, or Shari'a law, and contact defence attorneys (which are very uncommon in the region). These centres could also be affiliated with law schools in the region.

Independent Media Initiative: The AHDR notes that there are less than 53 newspapers per 1,000 Arab citizens compared with 285 papers per 1,000 people in developed countries, and that the Arab newspapers that do circulate tend to be of poor quality. Most news televisions programmes in the region are state-owned or controlled, and their quality is often poor, lacking analytical and investigative reporting. This deficit leads to a lack of public discourse and interest in prints media and limits the information available to the public. To counter this, the G-8 could.

- Sponsor exchange for prints and broadcast journalists.
- Sponsor training programmes for independent journalists.

- Provide scholarships for students to attend journalism schools in the region or abroad; fund programmes that would send journalists or journalism professors to hold training seminars on issues like election coverage or spend a semester teaching at school the regions.

Transparency/Anti-Corruption Efforts: The world has identified corruption as the single biggest obstacle to development, and in many GME countries it has become endemic. The G-8 could.

- Promote adoption of the G-8 Transparency and Anti-Corruption Principles.

- Publicly support the OECD/UNPD Middle East-North Africa initiative, through which senior government leaders, donors, IFIs, and NGOs discuss national strategies to fight corruption and strengthen government accountability.

- Launch one or more G-8 transparency pilots in the region.

Civil Society: Since genuine reform in the GME must be driven internally, and since the best means to promote reform is through representative organisations, the G-8 should encourage the development of effective civil society organisations in the region. The G-8 could.

- Encourage the region's governments to allow civil society organisations, including human rights and media NGOs' to operate freely without harassment or restrictions.

- Increase direct funding to democracy, human rights, media, women's and other NGOs in the region.
- Increase the technical capacity of NGOs in the region by increasing funding to domestic organisations (such as the UK's Westminister Foundation or the US National Endowment for Democracy) to provide training for NGOs on how to define a platform, lobby government, and development media and grassroots strategies to garner support. These programmes could also include exchanges and the creation of regional networks.
- Fund an NGO that would bring together legal or media expert from the region to draft annual assessments of judicial reform efforts or media freedom in the region. (This could follow the AHDR model 1).

II. Building a Knowledge Society

"Knowledge constitutes the road to development and liberation, especially in a world of intense globalisation."

Arab Human Development Report, 2002

The Greater Middle East region, once the cradle of scientific discovery and learning, has largely failed to keep up with today's knowledge-oriented world. The region's growing knowledge gap and continuing brain drain challenge its development prospects. Arab countries' output of books represent just 1.1 per cent of the world total (with religious books constituting over 15 per cent of this). Roughly one-fourth of all university graduates emigrate, and technology is largely imported. Five times as many books are translated into Greek (spoken by just 11mn people) as Arabic.

Building on education reform efforts already underway in the region, the G-8 could provide assistance to address the region's education challenges and help students acquire the skill needed to succeed in today's global marketplace.

Basic Education Initiative: Basic education in the region suffers from inadequate (and declining) public funding, increasing demand due to populations pressures, and cultural factors that limit access for girls. The G-8 could commit to a new GME Basic Education Initiative with the following components:

- **Literacy :** In 2003, the UN launched the literacy decade programme, under the theme "Literacy as Freedom". The G-8 literacy initiative would complement the UN programme through a focus on creating a literate generation in the Greatest Middle East over the next decade, with a goal of cutting in half the region's illiteracy rate by 2010. As with the UN programme, the G-8 initiative would target women and girls. Given them 65mn adults in the region are illiterate, the G-8 initiative could also focus on adult literacy and training with a variety of programmes, from outline curricula to teacher training.
- **Literate Corps:** To improve literacy among girls,

the G-8 could or expand teacher training institutes targeting women. At these institutes, female schoolteachers and educational specialists would then focus on reading and basic education for girls. The programme could employ the guidelines established in the Education for All programme coordinated by UNESCO, and the goal would be to train a "literacy Corps" of 10,000 female teachers by 2008.

- **Textbooks:** The AHDR notes a markage shortage of translation of basic books on philosophy, literature, sociology and the natural sciences, and makes note of the sorry state of libraries" in universities. To counter this deficit, each G-8 country could fund a programme to translate its "classics" in these fields, and where appropriate, countries, or publishers (in a public - private partnership) could reissue classic Arabic text that are now out of print. These books would then be donated to school, university and local libraries.

- **Discovery Schools Initiative:** Jordan has begun implementing its "discovery schools" initiative, in which new technology and teaching methods are employed are employed. The G-8 could support the expansion of this concept to other GME countries, providing funding and calling on support from the private sector.

- **Education Reform:** Before the G-8 Summit (in March or April), the US Middle East Partnership Initiative will sponsor a Middle East Education

Reforms Summit. This event will bring together reform-minded public, private sector, civic and community leaders from the region, along with their counterparts from the US and EU in order to identify common areas of concern and discuss methods for bridging education deficits. This event could be hosted as a G-8 event, as a way to build support for the GME initiative in the run-up to the summit.

Digital Knowledge Initiative: The region has the world's lowest level of internet access. Given the ever increasing stock of knowledge available on the Internet, and the growing importance of the internet to education and commerce, it is critical to bridge the "digital divide" between the GME and the rest of the world. The G-8 could launch public - private partnership to provide or expand computer access in schools throughout the GME, especially in remote areas. With the great diversity of wealth and infrastructure among countries in the region, and between rural and urban areas within the region's countries, in some areas it may be more appropriate to vide computer access in post offices, as has been done successfully in Russian towns and villages.

The project could initially focus on GME countries with the lowest Internet penetration (Iraq, Afghanistan, Pakistan, Yemen, Syria, Libya, Algeria, Egypt, Morocco) and would seek to wire as many schools/post offices as possible, funding permitting.

This initiative to wire schools in the region could

be coupled with the "Literacy Corps Initiative" described above: Institute teachers could train local teachers to develop curricula for online instruction, and the private sector could supply needed hardware. The computers could then be used by local teachers/ students, particularly in rural or poor areas

Business Education Initiative: In order to boost business educating throughout the region, the G-8 could establish partnerships between G-8 based business schools and educational institutions (universities or specialised institutes) in the region. G-8 countries could fund the placement of faculty and resources in these partnerships institutes, which would host specific educational programmes. These programmes could run the gamut from formal year - long graduate training to short courses on specific issues, such as preparing a business plan or a marketing strategy.

The Bahrain Institute of Banking and Finance, which has an American director and partnerships with several US universities, could be a model for such institutes.

III. Expanding Economic Opportunities

Closing the Greater Middle East regions prosperity gap will require an economic transformation similar in magnitude to that undertaken by the formerly communist countries of Central and Eastern Europe. Key to that transformation will be to unleash the region's private sector potential, especially small and medium enterprises which are the primary engines of economic growth and job creation. The growth of an entrepreneurial class in the GME would also be an important element in helping democracy and freedom flourish. The G-8 could commit following components:

- **Microfinance:** While some microfinance institutions exist in the region, entrepreneurs continue to face a large financing gap : only 5 per cent of the people seeking mircofinance receive it, and only 0.7 per cent of the total financing needed is actually provided. The G-8 could help fill this gap through microfinance, especially for- profit microfinance, focused primarily on women. For profit institutions are self sustaining and do not depend on external gramts of funds for continued operation and growth. We estimate that, assuming an average loan of $40mn, $500mn over years could help 1.2mn entrepreneurs help themselves out of poverty, 7,50,000 of whom could be women.

- **GME Finance Corporation:** The G-8 could agree to co-finance a corporation modelled on the International Finance Corporation to help incubate medium and larger-sized businesses, with an aim toward regional business integration. The corporation could be managed by a group of G-8 private sector leaders committed to applying their expertise in business development to the GME region.

- **GME Development Bank (GMED Bank):** The G-8, along with creditors in the GME region, could establish a new regional development institution modelled on the European Bank for Reconstruction and Development (EBRD) to help reforming countries finance basic development priorities. The new institution would pool the resources of wealthier GME nations and the G-8 to focus on improving access to education, health care, and basic infrastructure. The GMED Bank would also serve as a store of technical assistance and development knowledge for the GME. Lending (or grant - making) decisions would be governed by each borrower's ability to demonstrate measurable reform results.

Partnership for Financing Excellence: To advance reform of financial services in the region, and to better integrate the GME into the global financial system, the G-8 could offer a new partnership to reform leaders in the region. This partnership would aim to liberalise and expand financial services in the GME, by providing a basket of financial sector technical assistance and expertise focused on:

- Implementing reform plan that reduce state dominance of financial services;
- Removing barriers of cross-border financial transactions;
- Modernising banking services;
- Introducing, refining, and expanding market-oriented financial instruments and
- Building regulatory structures that encourage the liberalisation of financial services.

Trade Initiative: Intra-regional in the Middle East is extremely low, comprising just 6 per cent of all Arab trade. Most GME countries trade with countries outside the region, and have built preferential trade agreements far away rather than next door. As a result, tariff and non-tariff barriers have become the norm, while cross-border trade remains rare. The G-8 could commit to establish a new initiative designed to promote trade in the GME, comprising of these elements:

- **WTO Accession/Implementation and Trade Facilitation:** The G-8 could increase its emphasis on WTO accession and implementation for countries in the region[3]. Specific technical assistance programme would include providing in-country advisors on WTO accession and generating G-8 wide commitment to encouraging the accession process, including a focus on identifying and removing non-tariff barriers to trade. Once WTO accession is complete, the focus would move on to the signing of additional WTO commitment such as TRIPs and Government Procurement Agreement and linking continued technical assistance could also be linked to a G-8 - sponsored region-wide programme on customs facilitation and logistics to reduce administrative and physical barriers to intraregional trade.

- **Trade Hubs:** The G-8 would establish hubs in the region focused on improving intra-regional trade and customs practices. The hubs would provide a variety of services to support private sectors trade flows and business to business contact, including "one stop shopping" for foreign investors, linkages to customs offices to reduce transportation processing times, and unified regulations to ease entry and exit of goods and services from the region.

- **Business Incubator Zones (BIZ):** Building on the success of export processing zones and special trade zones in other regions, the G-8 could help establish specially designed zones in the GME that would encourage regional cooperation in the design, manufacturing and marketing of products. The G-8 could offer enhanced access to their markets for these products, and provide expertise in establishing the zones.

GME Economic Opportunities Forum: To encourage enhanced regional cooperation, the G-8 could establish a Middle East Economic Opportunity Forum, which would bring together top officials from the G-8 and GME (with possible side meetings of non-governmental officials and individuals from the business community) to discuss economic reforms issues. The forum could be based loosely on the APEC model, and would cover regional economic issues, including finance, trade and regulatory issues.

---

3. WTO Accession Applicants (WTO working party established): Algeria, Lebanon, Saudi Arabia and Yemen. WTO Accession Applicants (application not yet reviewed): Afghanistan, Iran, Libya and Syria. Observer Status Applicant: Iraq

APPENDIX II

THE TUNIS DECLARATION
issued at the 16th session of the Arab Summit, held in Tunis on May 22-23, 2004

We, the Leaders of the Arab States, meeting at the Summit Conference of the Arab League Council in its 16th ordinary session held in Tunis, the capital of the Republic of Tunisia, on May 22-23, 2004:

"Committed as we are to the principles upon which the League of Arab States was founded and to the objectives enunciated in its Charter, as well as to the noble universal values spelled out in the United Nations Charter and to all the instruments of international legality; - " Taking into account the new world changes and the challenges and stakes they generate;

"Determined to pursue efforts in order to strengthen the solidarity and cohesion of the Arab Nation, and to consolidate the Arab ranks, in the service of our primordial causes.

Declare the following:

1.1. The commitment of all international parties to materialise the principles of international legality and the UN resolutions pertaining to the Arab-Israeli conflict, without excluding any of the legal references of the peace process, constitutes the basis for a just, comprehensive and durable settlement to this conflict, in accordance with the Arab peace initiative and in implementation of the "Roadmap".

The international community should join its efforts so as to provide the necessary protection for the Palestinian people against the continuing acts of killing and deportation they are enduring, and also to put an end to the policy of assassination perpetrated by Israel against the Palestinian political leaders, to the siege imposed on the Palestinian people and their leadership, as well as to the aggressions targeting civilians without distinction. Joining these efforts would pave the way for the resumption of peace talks and would enable the brotherly Palestinian people to recover their legitimate rights, in the forefront of which the establishment of their independent state with East El-Quds as its capital, as well as the evacuation of all the Arab-occupied territories, including the occupied Syrian Golan and the Lebanese Chabâa Farms.

1.2. Achieving these legitimate objectives would provide propitious conditions for building confidence and for establishing a just, durable and comprehensive peace in the region, by convening an international conference aimed at ridding the Middle East region, including Israel, of the weapons of mass destruction. This will lay the foundations for a new era of entente, based on a mutual commitment to peace as a strategic choice, and will enable the Arab Nation and all countries in the region to focus their efforts on taking up the challenges confronting them and on pursuing the development action.

1.3. The Arab community is committed to support the Iraqi territorial integrity and to respect the sovereignty, independence and national unity of sisterly Iraq, and exhorts the Security Council to give a central and active role to the United Nations in Iraq in order to put an end to the occupation and prepare the ground for the transfer of power to the Iraqi people. This will make it possible to establish peace and stability and to launch the process of reconstruction in Iraq.

Entrusting an Arab troika (the current chairmanship, the previous chairmanship and the next chairmanship of the summit, along with the Arab League Secretary-General) with making the necessary contacts and following up the evolution of the situation in Iraq.

1.4. Reaffirming the Arab solidarity with sisterly Syria in the face of the American sanctions, and underlining the necessity to favour the logic of dialogue and mutual understanding in settling conflicts among states, so as to spare the region at this critical juncture further tension and instability.

1.5. Reaffirming the sovereignty of sisterly United Arab Emirates on its three islands and supporting all peaceful steps and initiatives that lead it to recover this sovereignty.

1.6. Reaffirming the Arab states' solidarity with the sisterly Republic of Sudan, and their determination to preserve its unity and territorial integrity and to reinforce all peace endeavours undertaken by the Sudanese government in conjunction with the international and regional parties.

1.7. Reaffirming the unity and sovereignty of the sisterly Republic of Somalia, and supporting the efforts aimed at achieving national conciliation, peace and stability in this country.

1.8. Reaffirming the determination to consecrate the national unity of the sisterly United Republic of Comoros, to preserve its territorial integrity and sovereignty, and to support all peace efforts in this country.

We also assert our firm determination:

2.1. To materialise our common will to develop the system of joint Arab action, through the Tunis Summit resolution to amend the Arab League Charter and to modernise its work methods and its specialised institutions, based on the various Arab initiatives and ideas included in the proposals put forward by the Secretary General as well as on a consensual and coherent vision and on a gradual and balanced approach.

2.2. To reaffirm our states' commitment to the humanitarian principles and the noble values of human rights in their comprehensive and interdependent dimensions, to the provisions of the various international conventions and charters, and to the Arab Human Rights Charter adopted by the Tunis Summit, as well as to the reinforcement of the freedom of expression, thought and belief and to the guarantee of the independence of the judiciary.

2.3. Endeavour, based on the Declaration on the process

of reform and modernisation in the Arab world, to pursue reform and modernisation in our countries, and to keep pace with the rapid world changes, by consolidating the democratic practice, by enlarging participation in political and public life, by fostering the role of all components of the civil society, including NGOs, in conceiving of the guidelines of the society of tomorrow, by widening women's participation in the political, economic, social, cultural and educational fields and reinforcing their rights and status in society, and by pursuing the promotion of the family and the protection of Arab youth.

2.4. To consolidate the comprehensive development programmes and intensify efforts aimed at promoting the educational systems, at disseminating knowledge and encouraging its acquisition, and at fighting illiteracy in order to ensure a better future for the Arab young generations.

2.5. To achieve economic complementarity among Arab States on the basis of the exchange of benefits and the interdependence of interests, and to endeavour to pursue the upgrading of the Arab economies by entrusting the Economic and Social Council with establishing a joint Arab economic and social action strategy, in such a way as to consolidate the competitiveness of the Arab economy and empower it to establish a solidarity-based partnership with the various economic groupings in the world.

2.6. To consecrate the values of solidarity and mutual assistance among the Arab states, as part of the Arab anti-poverty strategy adopted by the Tunis Summit, to mobilise all human potentialities in the Arab countries in support of the development efforts, and to endeavour to upgrade the economy of the least developed Arab countries and promote their development programmes.

2.7. Be prepared, as best as possible, to actively participate, at the level of governments, civil society and the private sector, in the World Summit on the Information Society whose second phase will be hosted by Tunisia in November 2005, so that this event will constitute an important opportunity to further promote the position of information and communication technologies in the Arab development plans, and reinforce the capacity of Arab countries to keep up with and contribute to the evolution witnessed in this sector which is one of the basic foundations of development.

2.8. To take appropriate measures to enable the Arab Organisation for Information and Communication Technologies to play its role in consolidating inter-Arab cooperation in this vital sector.

2.9. To strengthen the bonds of friendship between Arab countries and other countries of the world, and to establish a new approach for solidarity-based cooperation and partnership with them, based on our determination to consecrate dialogue among religions and cultures and to highlight the civilisational and humanist mission of Islam which calls for disseminating the values of tolerance, concord and peaceful coexistence among peoples and nations, and rejects hatred and discrimination.

2.10. To reaffirm the commitment of Arab States to pursue their contribution to the international efforts exerted to stand against and combat all forms of terrorism, avoid confusing Islam with terrorism and differentiate between legitimate resistance and terrorism.

2.11. To call for the holding of an international conference, under the auspices of the United Nations, in order to establish an international code of ethics for the fight against terrorism, while working to tackle the root causes of this phenomenon.

3. We express our deep thanks and high consideration to His Excellency President Zine El Abidine Ben Ali, President of the Republic of Tunisia, for his experience, insightfulness, and open-mindedness in managing our Summit proceedings. We are convinced that under his chairmanship of the Summit, the process of joint Arab action will witness further progress, and that the status of the Arab Nation among the nations of the world will be further reinforced.

Our thanks and appreciation also go to the Republic of Tunisia for having hosted the Summit Conference of the Arab League Council in its 16th ordinary session and for its meticulous preparation, in consultation with the Arab countries, in order to ensure optimum conditions for the organisation of the Summit. We also commend the efforts exerted by the Arab League Secretary General in this regard.

Tunis, May 22-23, 2004.

APPENDIX III

Broader Middle East/North Africa Partnership
Partnership for Progress and a Common Future with the Region of the Broader Middle East and North Africa

Sea Island

Georgia

1. We the leaders of the G8 are mindful that peace, political, economic and social development, prosperity and stability in the countries of the Broader Middle East and North Africa represent a challenge which concerns us and the international community as a whole. Therefore, we declare our support for democratic, social and economic reform emanating from that region.

2 The peoples of the Broader Middle East and North Africa have a rich tradition and culture of accomplishment in government, trade, science, the arts, and more. They have made many lasting contributions to human civilisation. We welcome recent statements on the need for reform from leaders in the region, especially the latest statement issued at the Arab League Summit in Tunis, in which Arab leaders expressed their determination "to firmly establish the basis for democracy." Likewise, we welcome the reform declarations of representatives of business and civil society, including those of Alexandria and the Dead Sea, Sana'a and Aqaba. As the leaders of the major industrialised democracies in the world, we recognise our special responsibility to support freedom and reform, and pledge our continuing efforts in this great task.

3. Therefore, we commit ourselves today to a Partnership for Progress and a Common Future with the governments and peoples of the Broader Middle East and North Africa. This partnership will be based on genuine cooperation with the region's governments, as well as business and civil society representatives to strengthen freedom, democracy, and prosperity for all.

4. The values embodied in the Partnership we propose are universal. Human dignity, freedom, democracy, rule of law, economic opportunity, and social justice are universal aspirations and are reflected in relevant international documents, such as the Universal Declaration on Human Rights.

5. In launching this Partnership, we adhere to the following principles:

5.1. Strengthening the commitment of the International Community to peace and stability in the region of the Broader Middle East and North Africa is essential.

5.2. The resolution of long-lasting, often bitter, disputes, especially the Israeli-Palestinian conflict, is an important element of progress in the region.

5.3. At the same time, regional conflicts must not be an obstacle for reforms. Indeed, reforms may make a significant contribution towards resolving them.

5.4. The restoration of peace and stability in Iraq is critical to the well-being of millions of Iraqis and the security of the region.

5.5. Successful reform depends on the countries in the

region, and change should not and cannot be imposed from outside.

5.6. Each country is unique and their diversity should be respected. Our engagement must respond to local conditions and be based on local ownership. Each society will reach its own conclusions about the pace and scope of change. Yet distinctiveness, important as it is, must not be exploited to prevent reform.

5.7. Our support for reform will involve governments, business leaders and civil societies from the region as full partners in our common effort.

5.8. Supporting reform in the region, for the benefit of all its citizens, is a long-term effort, and requires the G-8 and the region to make a generational commitment.

6. Our support for reform in the region will go hand in hand with our support for a just, comprehensive, and lasting settlement to the Arab- Israeli conflict, based upon UN Resolutions 242 and 338. We fully endorse the Quartet's Statement of May 4, 2004 and join the Quartet in its "common vision of two states, Israel and a viable, democratic, sovereign and contiguous Palestine, living side by side in peace and security." We support the work of the International Task Force on Palestinian Reform and the Ad Hoc Liaison Committee and urge all states to consider the assistance they may provide to their work. We welcome the establishment of the World Bank's Trust Fund and urge donors to contribute to this important initiative. We join in the Quartet's call for "both parties to take steps to fulfil their obligations under the roadmap as called for in UN

Security Council Resolution 1515 and previous Quartet statements, and to meet the commitments they made at the Red Sea Summits in Aqaba and Sharm el Sheikh." We reaffirm that a just, comprehensive, and lasting settlement to the Arab-Israeli conflict, including with respect to Syria and Lebanon, must comply with the relevant UN Security Council resolutions, including Resolution 425, which "Calls for strict respect for the territorial integrity, sovereignty and political independence of Lebanon within its internationally recognised boundaries."

7. We stand together united in our support for the Iraqi people and the fully sovereign Iraqi Interim Government as they seek to rebuild their nation. Iraq needs the strong support of the international community in order to realise its potential to be a free, democratic, and prosperous country, at peace with itself, its neighbours, and with the wider world. We welcome the unanimous approval of United Nations Security Council Resolution 1546 on Iraq, and we join in supporting the continued, expansive engagement of the United Nations in Iraq after the transfer of sovereignty, as circumstances permit. We pledge to provide support and assistance for the electoral process leading to national elections for the Transitional National Assembly no later than January 31, 2005. We are united in our desire to see the Multinational Force for Iraq, in accordance with the UNSCR 1546, succeed in its mission to help restore and maintain security, including protection of the United Nations presence, and to support humanitarian and reconstruction efforts.

We express our shared commitment, and urge others, to support the economic revitalisation of Iraq, focusing on priority projects identified by the Interim Government. We welcome the success of the recent International Reconstruction Fund Facility donors' conference in Doha, and commit to meeting before the next conference in Tokyo later this year to identify how each of us can contribute to the reconstruction of Iraq. Debt reduction is critical if the Iraqi people are to have the opportunity to build a free and prosperous nation. The reduction should be provided in connection with an IMF programme, and sufficient to ensure sustainability taking into account the recent IMF analysis. We will work with each other, within the Paris Club, and with non-Paris Club creditors, to achieve that objective in 2004. To help reestablish the ties that link Iraq to the world, we will explore ways of reaching out directly to the Iraqi people - to individuals, schools, and cities - as they emerge from decades of dictatorship and deprivation to launch the political, social, and economic rebirth of their nation.

8. The Partnership we launch today builds on years of support for reform efforts in the region through bilateral and multilateral cooperation programmes. The Euro-Mediterranean Partnership ("Barcelona Process"), the US Middle East Partnership Initiative, and the Japan-Arab Dialogue Initiative are examples of our strong commitment to supporting democratic and economic development. We are similarly committed to such progress in Afghanistan and Iraq through our multilateral reconstruction efforts. The Partnership we

propose will build on our ongoing engagement in the region.

9. The magnitude of the challenges facing the region requires a renewed commitment to reform and cooperation. Only by combining our efforts can we bring about lasting democratic progress. We welcome and support the work of other governments, institutions, and multilateral agencies that aim to assist the region's development.

10. Central to this new Partnership will be a "Forum for the Future," which will root our efforts in an open and enduring dialogue. The Forum will provide a framework at ministerial level, bringing together G-8 and regional Foreign, Economic, and other Ministers in an ongoing discussion on reform, with business and civil society leaders participating in parallel dialogues. The Forum will serve as a vehicle for listening to the needs of the region, and ensuring that the efforts we make collectively respond to those concerns.

11. Our efforts in the Partnership we commit to today focus on three areas:

11.1. In the *political sphere,* progress towards democracy and the rule of law entails instituting effective guarantees in the areas of human rights and fundamental freedoms, which notably imply respect for diversity and pluralism. This will result in cooperation, the free exchange of ideas, and the peaceful resolution of differences. State reform, good governance, and modernisation are also necessary ingredients for building democracy.

11.2. In the *social and cultural sphere,* education for all, freedom of expression, equality between men and women as well as access to global information technology are crucial to modernisation and prosperity. A better-educated workforce is a key to active participation in a globalised world. We will focus our efforts to reduce illiteracy and increase access to education, especially for girls and women.

11.3. In the *economic sphere,* creating jobs is the number one priority of many countries in the region. To expand opportunity, and promote conditions in which the private sector can create jobs, we will work with governments and business leaders to promote entrepreneurship, expand trade and investment, increase access to capital, support financial reforms, secure property rights, promote transparency and fight corruption. Promotion of intra-regional trade will be a priority for economic development of the Broader Middle East and North Africa.

12. The Partnership for Progress and a Common Future offers an impulse to our relationship with the Broader Middle East and North Africa region. As an expression of our commitment, we issue today an initial Plan of Support for Reform outlining current and planned activities to give life to this Partnership.

G-8 Plan of Support for Reform

We welcome the desire and commitment to continue reform and modernisation expressed by leaders in the region. Through consultation and dialogue with leaders and peoples in the region, and in response to reform priorities identified by the region, including by the Arab League, we have developed an initial plan of support for reform. The initiatives herein offer a broad range of opportunities from which governments, business, and civil society in the region can draw support as they choose. This will be a dynamic process based on mutual respect. It builds on our already strong bilateral and collective engagement with the region and is intended to expand and evolve over time. Today, in the spirit of partnership and in support of reform efforts in the region, we commit to:

1.1 Establish together with our partners a Forum for the Future to:

- Provide a ministerial framework for our ongoing dialogue and engagement on political, economic, and social reform in a spirit of mutual respect;
- Bring together in one forum foreign, economic and other ministers of the G-8 and the region on a regular basis;
- Serve as a collaborative vehicle for expanding our engagement in support of the region's reform efforts, in particular toward the enhancement of democracy and civic participation, rule of law, human rights and open market economy;
- Be accompanied by parallel business-to-business and civil society-to-civil society dialogues, whose participants will provide input on reforms and work with the Forum's member governments on implementation;

- Encourage cultural exchange and cooperation.

The inaugural meeting of the Forum for the Future was held in the Fall of 2004.

1.2 Launch a microfinance initiative to expand sustainable microfinance in the region and increase financing opportunities for the region's small entrepreneurs, especially women, including by:

- Establishing a Microfinance Consultative Group, managed by the World Bank's Consultative Group to Assist the Poor (CGAP), that would include G-8, regional, and other donors and partners, who would meet regularly to review microfinance progress, coordinate efforts, set benchmarks, help governments in the region establish a policy environment conducive to sustainable microfinance institutions, and exchange best practices;

- Working with CGAP to establish in the region a Best Practices Training Centre, which will concentrate on improving the policy and regulatory framework, disseminating best practice materials, building management capacity, and training a new generation of professional microfinance managers. The Centre would draw from the Microfinance Consultative Group's experience and guidelines;

- Launching pilot programmes in the region to help small entrepreneurs open or expand their businesses and create new jobs; the microfinance institutions would use the best practices center's training opportunities to train local managers, staff, and, if needed, government officials in "best practices;"

- In conjunction with the countries of the region, pledging to help over two million potential entrepreneurs to pull themselves out of poverty through microfinance loans over five years.

Jordan has offered to host the Best Practices Microfinance Training Centre, and Yemen has offered to host the first microfinance pilot programme.

1.3 Enhance support for efforts in the region, including through the appropriate multilateral institutions, to impart literacy skills to an additional 20 million people by 2015 with the aim of assisting governments in the region to achieve their objective of halving the illiteracy rate over the next decade (a target consistent with a goal of the January 2004 Beirut Conference on Education for All) including by:

- Training teachers in techniques, including on-line learning, that enhance the acquisition of literacy skills among school-aged children, especially girls, and of functional literacy skills among adults;
- Working to train, including through appropriate multilateral institutions, 100,000 teachers by 2009, with a particular focus on high-quality literacy skills;
- Providing teacher training through existing institutions and employing guidelines established

in the "Education for All" programmeme administered by UNESCO;

- Setting up and maintaining a regional network for sharing experience and best practices;
- Expanding and improving education opportunities for girls and women, including by providing assistance to help local communities have access to learning centres and schools;
- Supporting community-based, demand-led adult literacy programmes and programmes outside the formal education system that couple literacy courses with lessons on health, nutrition, and entrepreneurial skills.

Algeria and Afghanistan have offered to sponsor the literacy initiative.

1.4 **Enhance support for business, entrepreneurship, and vocational training programmes** to help young people, especially women, expand their employment opportunities, including by:

- Carrying out programmes, in alliance with business partners in our countries and in the region, to provide 250,000 young people with hands-on entrepreneurial training;
- Sponsoring or supporting seminars for outstanding executives, especially women, to enhance their skills through short-term business programmes and more focused, industry-specific sessions;

- Carrying out or sponsoring corporate apprenticeship programmes, in cooperation with local businesses and chambers of commerce, to increase internship opportunities for the region's young men and women;

- Encouraging exchanges of engineers and support for vocational training initiatives.

Bahrain and Morocco have offered to sponsor the entrepreneurship and vocational training initiative.

1.5 Establish with willing partners in the region a Democracy Assistance Dialogue that will, under the auspices of the Forum for the Future, bring together in a collaborative and transparent environment willing governments, civil society groups and other organisations from G-8, EU and others, and countries in the region to:

- Coordinate and share information and lessons learned on democracy programmes in the region, taking into account the importance of local ownership and each country's particular circumstances;

- Work to enhance existing democracy programmes or initiate new programmes;

- Provide opportunities for participants to develop joint activities, including twinning projects;

- Promote and strengthen democratic institutions and processes, as well as capacity-building;

- Foster exchanges with civil society groups and other organisations working on programmes in the region.
- Turkey, Yemen, and Italy will co-sponsor the Democracy Assistance Dialogue and host the first meeting later in 2004.

1.6 Establish a Broader Middle East and North Africa Private Enterprise Development Facility at the International Finance Corporation (IFC) to assist the region's efforts to improve the business and investment climate and increase the financing options for the region's small and medium-sized businesses (SMEs), including by:

- Combining and expanding in terms of funding and geographic reach the IFC's two regional facilities to create a new USD$100 million facility that will cover the entire region, funded by contributions from G-8 countries, countries within the region, and other donors. Our Finance Ministers will convene a meeting to this end with interested countries;
- Leveraging existing expertise, experience, and financial resources of the IFC;
- Providing technical assistance to interested countries working on improving their business and investment climate;
- Encouraging the IFC to increase the focus of its regional investment portfolio on SMEs;
- Providing an appropriate mix of technical

assistance and financial instruments.

1.7 Establish a regional "Network of Funds" that would bring together representatives from development institutions based in the region and from international financial institutions for the purposes of:

- Coordinating better existing programmes and resources;
- Supporting through technical assistance regional efforts to build institutional capacity and improve the investment climate;
- Exploring the voluntary pooling of new and existing resources to target financing to SMEs and large cross-border projects.

1.8 Establish with partners in the region a Task Force on Investment, comprising business leaders from the G-8 and the region, including from the Arab Business Council, to assist the region's efforts to improve the investment climate, including by:

- Identifying impediments to investment;
- Recommending concrete proposals for change, and quantifying where possible likely benefits;
- Working with countries in the region interested in pursuing reforms and supporting their reform efforts;
- Reviewing and reporting on progress of reform in the region.

***

In addition to the foregoing initiatives, we will seek opportunities to increase coordination of our respective ongoing activities that are available to support reform in the region. We commit to intensify and in partnership and dialogue with governments, business, and civil society, expand these already strong individual and collective engagements. These activities respond to reform priorities identified by the region, including by the Arab League Summit Tunis Declaration, the Alexandria Library Statement, the Sana'a Declaration, and the Arab Business Council Declaration.

Deepening Democracy and Broadening Participation in Political and Public Life

Tunis Declaration: "We...assert our firm determination... to pursue reform and modernisation in our countries and keep pace with rapid global change by fostering democratic practice; by broadening participation in political and public life; by strengthening the role of all components of civil society, including NGOs; by envisioning the society of tomorrow; by expanding women's participation in political, economic, social, cultural, and educational fields; by enhancing their rights and status in society; and by pursuing the promotion of family and the protection of Arab youth."

Alexandria Library Statement: "Democracy is a system in which freedom is both fundamental and paramount. As such it yields true sovereignty for the people who govern themselves by means of political pluralism, ensuring regular transition of governing authority. It is a system that is founded upon a total respect for the rights of the people to freedom of thought, organisation and expression."

Sana'a Declaration: "Democratic systems protect the rights and interests of everybody without discrimination, especially the rights and interests of disadvantaged and vulnerable groups... The basics of democratic systems are reflected in periodically elected legislatures, representing the citizens in a fair way and ensuring their full participation, in executive bodies that are responsible and committed to principles of good governance and in an independent judiciary..."

Arab Business Council Declaration: ". . . Improving the standards of living in the Arab world necessitates focusing on . . . Respecting the rule of law and enhancing transparency . . . reducing red-tape and corruption . . . Promoting adequate institutional and legal mechanisms . . . Developing the Arab judicial system . . . [and] Activating the role of women and youth in society."

2.1 Supporting efforts to ensure free and transparent elections by cooperating with willing countries, including by assisting independent election commissions, and voter registration programmes and supporting civic awareness programmes, with a particular emphasis on women voters. Representative G-8 activities include:

- Canada is supporting preparations, including voter registration, for free and transparent elections in Afghanistan.
- The European Union is supporting the preparation

of Palestinian elections by providing international elections experts and financial assistance to the independent Palestinian Central Election Commission.

- France is providing support for parliamentary elections in Yemen in order to assist the authorities in strengthening the democratisation process in the country.
- Italy provides technical assistance to, and support of, electoral processes in Afghanistan and Yemen.

2.2 **Supporting and encouraging parliamentary exchanges and training** to build the capacity of the region's parliaments and consultative bodies, particularly with regard to drafting legislation, implementing legislative and legal reforms, and representing constituents. Representative G-8 activities include:

- The United Kingdom has a three-year project in Bahrain to improve the capacity of parliament, including a youth parliament.

2.3 **Supporting regional efforts to expand women's participation in political, economic, social, cultural, and educational fields and by enhancing their rights and status in society** including by supporting training for women interested in running for elective office or establishing or operating an NGO; and bringing together women in leadership positions from G-8 countries and the region, including in workshops. Representative G-8 activities include:

- Canada supports Egyptian organisations working on issues of basic education and employment to include focus on the fuller participation of girls and women.

- France supports the development of women's rights in Morocco, Algeria, Tunisia, Jordan, Palestinian Territories and Lebanon in cooperation with UN Development Fund for Women (UNIFEM), in order to strengthen efforts to develop their participation in society and to make them aware of their rights.

- Germany is supporting partners in Jordan, Morocco, and Yemen in promoting gender equality, including through increasing women's access to professional opportunities and participation in public life.

- Japan is providing support to empower women in Jordan, Egypt, and the Palestinian Territories in order to enhance their leadership role in the society.

- The United States is funding regional women's campaign schools in North Africa, the Levant, and the Gulf that provide political skills training and assist women who wish to enter into electoral politics.

2.4 Assisting the region in pursuing judicial reforms and in ensuring an independent judiciary, including by: supporting judicial exchanges and workshops as well as training for judges, attorneys, and law students; providing technical assistance for judicial administration and legal code reforms; and the establishment of grassroots legal aid centres. Representative G-8 activities include:

- The European Union is supporting the establishment of a Palestinian Constitutional Court and a National Legal Training Institute, thereby contributing to judicial reform.
- France is developing a specific cooperation programme in Syria in order to respond to the demand of the authorities to reform the administrative and judicial systems.
- Italy supports in Afghanistan reconstruction of the judicial system, a survey on the state of law, establishment of itinerant courts, and training of judges and lawyers.
- The United Kingdom is strengthening the capacity of Jordanian national institutions, including the judiciary, to tackle family violence, child abuse, and sexual assault through a rights-based approach.

2.5 Supporting the region's efforts to reinforce the freedom of expression, thought and belief, and to encourage an independent media, including by: sponsoring exchanges, training, and scholarships for journalists. Representative G-8 activities include:

- France is helping to modernise the national radio in Lebanon through training and scholarships for journalists and to create a specific academic programme in the Egyptian university to train young journalists.

- The United Kingdom is supporting a three-year media training project with BBC World Service Trust in Syria, Lebanon, Egypt, and Morocco.

2.6 Encouraging the region's efforts to foster the democratic process, promote good governance, transparency and anti-corruption efforts, including by: encouraging adoption and implementation of the United Nations Convention against Corruption; technical assistance for the reform and modernisation of public financial management and procurement practices and for efforts to combat money laundering and terrorist finance. Representative G-8 activities include:

- Italy supports electronic government, including the development of e-procurement and e-accounting systems in public administration in Jordan and Tunisia.

- Germany is supporting partners in Yemen and Mauritania in reforming and modernising public financial management systems including through capacity-building of national, regional, and local government and parliamentary bodies.

- Japan is providing assistance through UNDP for the capacity-building of the administration of the Palestinian Authority, including its Prime Minister's Office.

- The United Kingdom is supporting a major programme of public administration and civil service reform for the Palestinian Authority, which aims to restructure and streamline the Palestinian Authority to meet the needs of a modern democratic state.

2.7 Supporting efforts to strengthen the role of all components of civil society, including NGOs in the region's reform processes, including by: providing assistance to strengthen the participation of all segments of society, supporting the efforts of institutions to strengthen the foundations of citizenship; encouraging exchanges among civil society organisations, including labour unions and collaborating on cultural projects and programmes. Representative G-8 activities include:

- The European Union supports the Arab Women's Organisation and the Jordanian Women's Union.
- France is financing social development funds in Morocco, Tunisia, and the Palestinian Territories, specifically designed to help NGOs, associations, and communities, to develop small social development projects that respond directly to the basic needs of the population and enhance their capacities to play a leading role in the development of the country at the local level.

Building a Knowledge Society to Combat Illiteracy and Advance Educational and Technological Systems

Tunis Declaration: "We also assert our firm determination...to...intensify efforts aimed at the development and progress of educational systems, at disseminating knowledge and encouraging its acquisition, and at combating illiteracy in order to ensure a better tomorrow for future generations of Arab youth.

Alexandria Library Statement: "Participants recommend . . . eradicating illiteracy - especially among women - within a ten-year period... acquiring, spreading, and producing knowledge... to achieve (the building of) a society of knowledge... revitalise civil and governmental translation institutions on two fronts: translations from Arabic to all recognised languages and from all languages to Arabic... modernise the information technology infrastructure in the Arab world."

Sana'a Declaration: "The practice of democracy and human rights and enhancing their understanding require overcoming potential threats to the form and substance of democracy, including... inadequate education."

Arab Business Council Declaration: "Governments need to take additional measures to improve the efficiency and quality of the education offered in their educational institutions... better align the knowledge and skill outputs of their educational systems with the changing and evolving needs of the global economy... Expand the capacity for knowledge acquisition by greater investment in IT infrastructure... "

3.1 Assisting countries interested in improving and reforming their education systems, including by: supporting efforts to improve the quality of education, fostering community participation in education, increasing the planning capacity of education ministries, facilitating community partnerships; and supporting construction and rehabilitation of schools. Representative G-8 activities include:

- Canada supports the education reform strategy of the Jordanian Ministry of Education to re-engineer primary and secondary education to meet the needs of the knowledge economy.

- Germany is assisting partners in Egypt, Jordan, Yemen, and the Palestinian Territories in improving national basic education systems, including through the enlargement of existing and the construction of new elementary schools.

- Italy supports a development programmeme for promotion of Education for All, and training graduates in Afghanistan and Libya.

- Japan is providing support to construct 30 primary and secondary schools in Yemen, which will benefit about 18,000 children.

- The United Kingdom has provided long-term support to the Egyptian Government to help them re-orientate their nation-wide adult literacy programme towards a demand-driven community-based approach.

- The United States is sponsoring "partnership schools" to enhance the quality of primary and secondary education, and conducting teacher training and providing classroom materials for early childhood education in Morocco, Tunisia, Oman, and Qatar.

3.2 Building on the rich cultural heritage of the region, increase availability of and access to textbooks and regional and world literature, including by: supporting local capacity in textbook publishing and translation; training teachers in new methods; and supporting the re-issuing of the region's classic texts. Representative G-8 activities include:

- Japan is supporting school textbook publishing in Yemen, through providing printing equipment which has the capacity to print 10 million textbooks a year.
- The United States is funding the translation of eighty children's book titles and accompanying teachers' manuals for school libraries in Jordan, Bahrain, and Lebanon, as well as American book translation programmes in Egypt and Jordan.

3.3 Assisting the region in enhancing its digital knowledge including by public-private partnerships to provide or expand computer access, supporting the introduction of innovative teaching methods to classrooms, integrating computer-based technology into curricula, and supporting "e-government" initiatives. Representative G-8 activities include:

- Canada supports the efforts of the Jordanian Ministry of Education to introduce and integrate information and communication technology into the national education system.

***

Accelerating Economic Development, Creating Jobs, Empowering the Private Sector, and Expanding Economic Opportunities

Tunis Summit Declaration: "We also assert our firm determination...To endeavour to pursue the upgrading of Arab economies...in such a way as to strengthen the competitiveness of the Arab economy and empower it to establish a solidarity-based partnership with the various global economic blocs."

Alexandria Library Statement: "In a young and rising Arab world, employment of youth, quality of education, social services and programmes supporting SMEs should be basic elements of the concept of reform...Develop SME and micro credit programmes to deal with unemployment giving females the full opportunity to access financing... Modernise Arab financial sectors generally, and banking sectors specifically, encouraging the establishment of large banking entities and modernisation of Arab capital markets... Resolve problems that hinder investment and remove obstacles to Arab and foreign investment... enable Arab countries to effectively join the World Trade Organisation [and] positively integrate in the global economy by increasing exports of goods and services..."

Sana'a Declaration: "The private sector is a vital partner in strengthening the foundations of democracy and human rights; it has a responsibility to work with governments and civil society to enhance progress."

Arab Business Council Declaration: "In order for

entrepreneurship to thrive, policy makers need to create environments that allow market forces to freely interplay, foster stability, and a high degree of predictability in order to enable investors to make long-term decisions... [including by] Enhancing accountability and securing full protection of property rights... Removing restrictions on foreign investment... Attaining a higher degree of global economic integration through trade liberalisation schemes, both in goods and services [and] adopting trade policies that are based on internationally-agreed rules and practices..."

4.1 Supporting vocational training programmes to expand job opportunities for the region's youth, including by: sponsoring continuing education programmes and training for workshops instructors and master craftsmen. Representative G-8 activities include:

- Canada supports the development of centres in the Palestinian Territories providing a range of technical and vocational training opportunities for Palestinian women to improve their economic situation.
- The European Union supports the Euro-Med Youth Programme, which has funded more than 600 projects and enabled 14,000 young people and youth leaders to participate in international youth mobility activities in the region.
- Germany is assisting partners in Algeria, Egypt, Iran, Lebanon, Morocco, Tunisia, Yemen, and the

Palestinian Territories in developing new job-oriented approaches for apprenticeship training to enable the region's youth to acquire better qualifications for wage-based or self-employed activities.

- Japan is providing technical assistance for an automobile maintenance project in Saudi Arabia contributing to building capacity for 600 workers.
- The United States is supporting nine Junior Achievement student chapters, directing the business internship programme for Arab women, and administering seminars for executives and mid-level managers in Bahrain, Egypt, Oman, Lebanon, UAE, Qatar, Saudi Arabia, Kuwait, and Morocco.

4.2 Supporting development of small and medium-sized enterprises, including through: assistance programmes, targeted loan programmes, and technical assistance to improve the policy and regulatory framework. Representative G-8 activities include:

- Germany is supporting Algeria, Egypt, Lebanon, Morocco, Tunisia, Yemen and the Palestinian Territories in enhancing the competitiveness of small and medium sized enterprises, including through loan programmes, training and the improvement of regulatory frameworks.
- The European Union supports a social fund for development in Egypt, assisting 25,000 new enterprises creating 95,000 jobs and helping 2,100

individuals with micro-credits for income generating activities.

- Italy supports financing for Small and Medium Enterprises in the Palestinian Territories, Egypt, Algeria, Iran, Jordan, Tunisia, and Pakistan.

4.3 Facilitating remittance flows from communities overseas to help families and small entrepreneurs, including by: encouraging the reduction of the cost of remittance transfers, and the creation of local development funds for productive investments; improving access by remittance recipients to financial services; and enhancing coordination. Representative G-8 activities include:

- Italy supports remittances transfer facilitation in Morocco.

4.4 Supporting efforts in the region to create fair, secure, and well-functioning property rights systems, including by: technical assistance for policy and regulatory reform and the improvement of property registries. Representative G-8 activities include:

- Italy supports projects for social and economic reform with the involvement of local authorities in the Palestinian Territories.

4.5 Promoting financial excellence and supporting efforts in the region to integrate its financial sector into the global financial system, including by: providing technical assistance to modernise financial services, and to introduce and expand market-oriented financial instruments; working with financial authorities to support good economic governance, including anti-corruption and anti-money laundering efforts. Representative G-8 Activities include:

- The United Kingdom is strengthening economic and financial management in Yemen by helping the Ministry of Finance implement a new budget formulation, execution, and monitoring system.
- The United States, through the Partnership for Financial Excellence, is training bank supervisors, placing resident advisors, and supporting private-sector volunteers providing technical assistance to commercial banks, central banks, and capital markets in Morocco, Jordan and Egypt; regional activities are open to all cooperating countries in the region.

4.6 Assisting regional efforts to remove barriers to investment, increase investment, and stimulate economic reforms, including by: providing technical assistance to improve investment climates; offering training for officials on investor rights; facilitating investment opportunities, including through investment treaties; and supporting work under the new OECD/UNDP Middle East-North Africa Initiative on investment. Representative G-8 Activities include:

- In the context of the Barcelona process, the European Union supports the establishment of a Euro-Mediterranean Free Trade Agreement with a view to fostering regional economic integration, enhanced trade flows and increased investments towards and within the region.

- Canada supports Tunisia and Algeria in their efforts to advance strategic regulatory reforms and to promote private sector and investment infrastructure as they develop open economies.

4.7 Supporting the region's efforts to achieve economic integration, promote intra-regional trade, and expand trade opportunities in global markets, including by: providing technical assistance for accession to the WTO; supporting intraregional trade agreements; sponsoring regional programmes on trade facilitation; and facilitating development of local chambers of commerce. Representative G-8 Activities include:

- France, together with the European Commission, supports the Euro-Mediterranean Action Plan on Trade and Investment Facilitation established in March 2002 that aims to modernise customs, promote foreign investments, assist applicants in the WTO accession process, and support a regional free trade agreement before 2010.

- Germany is supporting partners in Algeria, Lebanon, Jordan, Morocco, Tunisia, and the Palestinian Territories in implementing free trade agreements, facilitating WTO accession or supporting local chambers of commerce.

- Japan is assisting the Foreign Trade Training Center in Egypt, which has been established to provide trade-related capacity building of business people.

- The United States is providing technical assistance

to: reach the goal of a Middle East Free Trade Area by 2013; support the accession of Algeria, Saudi Arabia, and Yemen to the WTO; aid seven countries in complying with Trade and Investment Framework Agreement; and enable Jordan, Morocco, and Bahrain to take advantage of their free trade agreements with the United States.

References

I. Background to the "Reform" Initiative

1. "Reconsidering Saudi Arabia", Editorial, *Washington Post,* November 11, 2001.

2. Gerges, Fawaz : "Saudi Arabia Must Stand Up to Bin Laden", *LA Times,* November 21, 2001.

3. Downloaded from : www.whitehouse.gov

4. *ibid.*

5. *ibid.*

6. Gordon, Philip H. "Bush's Middle East Vision", Survival, Vol. 45, No.1, Spring 2003, p. 155; henceforth *Gordon.*

7. *Gordon,* p. 158.

8. *ibid.*

9. Quoted in : Cicincione, Joseph : "Origins of Regime Change in Iraq", Carnegie Endowment for International Peace, Proliferation Brief, Vol.6, No.5, March 19, 2003.

10. *ibid.*

11. *ibid.*

12. *Arab Human Development Report – 2002 :* Creating Opportunities for Future Generations, UNDP &

Arab Fund for Economic and Social Development; downloaded from : www.undp.org/rbas.

13. Downloaded from : www.state.gov/secretary/rm/2002

14. Middle East and North Africa Briefing, *International Crisis Group(ICG) Briefing*, Brussels/Amman, June 7, 2004, p. 3; henceforth *ICG Briefing*.

15. *ibid.*

16. Downloaded from : www.state.gov

17. *Arab Human Development Report-2003 :* Building a Knowledge Society, UNDP and Arab Fund for Economic and Social Development; downloaded from : www.undp.org/rbas; henceforth *AHDR* 2003.

18. *AHDR 2003*, p. *1.*

19. *ibid.*

20. *AHDR 2003*, p. 2.

21. *AHDR 2003*, p. 3.

22. *ibid.*

23. *AHDR 2003*, Executive Summary, Middle East Economic Survey (MEES), November 3, 2003, p. D7; henceforth *MEES Summary*.

24. *MEES Summary*, p. D9.

25. *MEES Summary*, p. D10-11.

26. Quoted in : *ICG Briefing*, p. 2.

II. The Greater Middle East Initiative (GMEI)

1. English translation printed as "G-8's Middle East Vision", in *MEES*, February 24, 2004.
2. Quoted in : Wright, Robin and Kessler, Glen : "Bush Aims for 'Greater Mideast' Plan", *Washington Post,* February 9, 2004.
3. *ibid.*
4. *ibid.*
5. Quoted in : *ICG Briefing,* p. 4.
6. Ottaway, Marina and Carothers, Thomas : "The Greater Middle East Initiative : Off to a False Start", Carnegie Endowment for International Peace, *Policy Brief,* March 29, 2004.
7. Quoted in : Debieuvre, Luc : "One May Prefer Democrats to Smoking Guns", *Gulf News,* Dubai, March 5, 2004.
8. *ibid.*
9. Brzezinski, Zbigniew : "Bush's Initiative : The Wrong Way to Sell Democracy to the Arab World", *Gulf News,* Dubai, March 9, 2004.
10. Quoted in : Almezel, Mohammed : "Full Democracy Not Possible in Gulf Region in Foreseeable Future, Says British Author", *Gulf News,* March 1, 2004.
11. *ibid.*

III. Response of the Arab World to the GMEI

1. Imam, Ghassan : "The Real Threat to Arab Democracy", *Asharq Al-Awsat*, London; translation printed in *Mideast Mirror*, October 16, 2002.

2. Huwaidi, Fahmi : "The Need for Change", *Al-Ahram*, Cairo; translation printed in *MEES*, June 9, 2003, p. C3.

3. Noureddin, Satie : "Entertaining Spectacle", *Al-Safir*, Beirut; translation printed in *Mideast Mirror*, March 5, 2004.

4. Hamadeh, Ali : "Crisis-ridden", *Al-Nahar*, Beirut; translation printed in *Mideast Mirror*, March 5, 2004.

5. Neemat, Salameh : "Pretence of Conflict", *Al-Hayat*, London; translation printed in *Mideast Mirror*, March 11, 2004.

6. Said, Abdelmoniem : "Preoccupation", *Al-Watan*, Abha, Saudi Arabia; translation printed in *Mideast Mirror*, March 22, 2004.

7. Itani, Hussam : "Approaching the Event Horizon," *Al-Safir*, Beirut; translation printed in *Mideast Mirror*, January 14, 2004.

8. Samaha, Joseph: "Arab Success", *Al-Safir*, Beirut; translation printed in *Mideast Mirror*, March 22, 2004.

9. Hafiz, Salaheddin : "Reform Programmes", *Al-Ahram;* translation printed in *Mideast Mirror*, May 26, 2004.

10. Hroub, Khaled : "A Case of US Amnesia", *Al-Rai*, Amman; translation printed in *Mideast Mirror*, February 18, 2004.

11. Hussain, Mushahid : "Goodbye to US Idea of 'Greater Middle East", *Gulf News*, March 17, 2004.

12. Zehra, Nasim : "Pakistan Not Part of Middle East", *Gulf News*, March 12, 2004.

13. Quoted in : Roumani, Rhonda; "Arab World Leery of American 'Reform", *The Daily Star*, Beirut, June 5, 2004.

14. Quoted in : "The Initiative Lacks Credibility", *The Guardian*, London, March 11, 2004.

15. Hroub, Khaled, *op.cit.*

16. Al-Shihabi, Said : "The Real Democracy Debate", *Al-Quds Al-Arabi*, London; translation printed in *Mideast Mirror*, November 21, 2003.

17. Wardam, Bater Mohd. Ali : "A Faulty US Design", Al-Dustour, Amman; translation printed in *Mideast Mirror*, February 17, 2004

18. Ahmad, Abdul Hamid : "Arab Reforms – a Public Demand, Not US Initiative", *Gulf News*, Dubai, March 8, 2004.

19. El Amrani, Issandr : "The Next Big Thing", *Cairo Times*, December 12-25, 2002; downloaded from www.cairotimes.com/news

20. *ibid.*

21. Quoted in *ICG Briefing*, p. 6.

22. Fergany, Nader : "Ghosts of Abu Ghraib", , *Al-Ahram Weekly*, May 20-26, 2004; downloaded from www.weekly.ahram.org.eg/print/2004/691/op65.htm

23. Al-Shihabi, Said : "Revived Proposal", *Al-Quds Al-Arabi*, London; translation printed in *Mideast Mirror*, November 21, 2003.

24. Alshateri, Albadr : "Bush and Democracy in the Middle East", *Gulf News*, January 23, 2004.

25. "Reforms Overdue in the Arab World", Editorial, *Gulf News*, March 7, 2004.

26. Ahmad, Abdul Hamid, *op.cit.*

27. Zaatra, Yasser : "Reform Again", *Al-Dustoor*, Amman; translation printed in *Mideast Mirror*, May 24, 2004.

28. Baroud, Ramzy: "Reform as Euphemism for Stagnation", *Arab News*, Jeddah, June 11, 2004

29. El-Effendi, Abdelwahab : "Tardy Realisation"; *Al-Quds Al-Arabi*, translation printed in *Mideast Mirror*, December 19, 2003.

30. Ibrahim, Mohammed : "No Democracy without Democrats"; *Al-Nahar*, Beirut; translation printed in *Mideast Mirror*, February 19, 2004.

31. Al-Ghabra, Nazim Shafik : "Endless Talk", *Al-Rai Al-Aam*, Kuwait; translation printed in *Mideast Mirror*, March 11, 2004.

32. Al-Maghlooth, Ghazi : Saudi Elections : Winds of Change, *Al-Watan*; translation printed in *Saudi Gazette*, Jeddah, October 20, 2003.

33. Noureddin, Satie : "Half a Step in a Journey of a Thousand Miles", *Al-Safir*; Beirut; translation printed in *Mideast Mirror*, October 15, 2003.

34. Al-Hamad, Turki : "A Small but Revolutionary Breakthrough", *Asharq Al-Awsat*, London; translation printed in *Mideast Mirror*, October 21, 2003.

35. Hamadeh, Ali : "Crisis-ridden", *Al-Nahar*; translation printed in *Mideast Mirror*, March 5, 2004.

IV. Official Arab Reform Initiatives

1. "Egypt Floats Own Idea for Arab Reform", *Times of Oman*, Muscat, March 2, 2004.

2. *ibid.*

3. Sharaf, Ayman : "A Reform Conference to Avoid any Significant Change", *Gulf News*, March 16, 2004.

4. *ibid.*

5. *ibid.*

6. Downloaded from www.eemonha.com/archives

7. *ibid.*

8. Speech circulated by Embassy of Qatar, Muscat, vide note No. : 5/3/1/-663, dated June 5, 2004.

9. Downloaded from : www.tunisiaonline.com

V. GMEI Revised : The Broader Middle East and North Africa Partnership [BMEP]

1. Office of the Press Secretary, the White House, June 9, 2004, downloaded from : www.whitehouse.gov
2. Wittes, Tamara Cofman : "The New US Proposal for a Greater Middle East Initiative : An Evaluation", *The Brookings Institution*, Middle East Memo #2, May 10, 2004; "G-8 Revises Plan to Blunt Arab Criticism", *Gulf News*, June 4, 2004; and *ICG Briefing*, pp. 7-10.
3. Quoted in *ICG Briefing*, p. 8.
4. "G-8 Plan of Support for Reform", June 9, 2004, downloaded from : www.whitehouse.gov
5. Snow, Charles : "Onward to Sea Island", *MEES*, June 14, 2004.
6. Quoted in *ibid.*
7. *ICG Briefing*, p. 10.
8. "A Start on Democracy", Editorial, *Washington Post*, April 28, 2004.
9. Young, Michael : "Without Outside Compulsion, Arab Reform is a Pipe Dream", *Daily Star*, Beirut, June 10, 2004.
10. *ibid.*
11. Wittes, Tamara Cofman : "Seize the Moment for

Arab Reform", *Daily Star*, June 17, 2004.

12. "A Positive Turn at the G-8 Summit", Editorial, *Al-Watan*; translation printed in *Mideast Mirror*, June 11, 2004.

13. El-Effendi, Abdel Wahab : "A Win against Democracy", *Al-Quds Al-Arabi*; translation printed in *Mideast Mirror*, June 14, 2004.

14. Samaha, Joseph : "The worst of both worlds", *Al-Safir*, Beirut; translation printed in *Mideast Mirror*, June 8, 2004.

15. Baroud, Ramzy, *op.cit.*

16. Hetata, Sherif : "Which democracy?", *Al-Ahram* weekly, issue No. 694, June 10-16, 2004; downloaded from www.weekly.ahram.org.eg

17. Brinkley, Joel: "US Slows Bid to Advance Democracy in the Arab World," *New York Times*, December 5, 2004.

18. Quoted in *ibid.*

19. Quoted in: Landay, Jonathan L.: "Arab-Israeli Dispute at Top of Reform Talk," *The Miami Herald*, December 12, 2004.

20. Quoted in *ibid.*

21. Quoted in *ibid.*

22. Quoted in *ibid.*

23. Shelby, David: "Middle East Forum for the Future

Produces Solid Initiatives," dated December 13, 2004, downloaded from http://usinfo.state.gov .

24. Quoted in *ibid*.

25. Quoted in: "Forum for the Future: A Non-constraining Dialogue Space, Moroccan Government Spokesman," dated December 11, 2004, downloaded from: http://www. arabicnews.com .

26. Noureddin, Satie: "An Unsuccessful Appearance," *Al-Safir*, Beirut; translation printed in *Mideast Mirror*, December 13, 2004.

27. Al-Ajami, Fawaz: "Dangerous Conference," *Al-Sharq*, Doha; translation printed in *Mideast Mirror*, December 13, 2004.

28. Al-Nuaimi, Abdelrahman: "Demands of the Age," *Al-Sharq*, Doha; translation printed in *Mideast Mirror*, December 14, 2004.

VI. The Content and Direction of Middle East Reform: Issues of Political Participation and "Islam" in the Reformed Polity

1. Quoted in : El-Effendi, Abdel Wahab : "The End of the Road for Arab Police States", *Al-Quds Al-Arabi*, London; translation printed in *Mideast Mirror*, August 15, 2003.

2. *ibid.*

3. Khashogji, Jamal : "Democracy Must Spring from Within", *Al-Watan*, Abha, Saudi Arabia; translation

printed in *Mideast Mirror*, December 24, 2003.

4. Satloff Robert : "The Greater Middle East Partnership : A Work Still Very Much in Progress", The Washington Institute for Near East Policy, *Policy Watch*, No. 836, February 25, 2004.

5. Zakaria, Fareed : "How to Save the Arab World", *Newsweek*, December 24, 2001.

6. Quoted in : "Wolfowitz on Democracy in the Mideast", *BusinessWeek online*, December 23, 2002.

7. *ibid.*

8. Saleh, Ahmad Abbas : "The Twin Challenges of Democracy and Education", *Asharq Al-Awsat*; translation in *Mideast Mirror*, June 16, 2003.

8 a. Makki, Yusif : "On the Road to Arab Reform", *Al-Watan*; translation printed in *Mideast Mirror*, April 8, 2004.

9. Harb, Dr. Usama Al-Ghazali : "The Need for Internal Arab Reform", *Al-Ahram*; translation printed in *MEES*, July 15, 2002.

10. Al-Rashid, Madhawi : "The Limits of Saudi Reform", *Al-Quds Al-Arabi*, London; translation printed in *Mideast Mirror*, January 15, 2004.

11. Al-Kabalan, Marwan : "Iraq is the Test for Greater Mideast Plan", *Gulf News*, March 5, 2004.

12. Benard, Cheryl : "Civil Democratic Islam – Partners, Resources and Strategies", National Security

Research Division, *RAND*, 2003, henceforth *Benard.*

13. *Benard*, p. (ix).

14. *ibid.*

15. *Benard*, p. (x).

16 *Benard*, p. (x-xii).

17. *Benard*, p. 25.

18. *Benard*, p. 28.

19. The Indian authority on Islamic history and politics Yoginder Sikand, has provided a detailed critique of Benard's monograph in his article : "Civic Democratic Islam", *www.outlookindia.online*, June 4, 2004; henceforth Sikand.

20. *Sikand*, p. 7.

21. Hurd, Elizabeth Shakman : "Secularism and Democracy in the Middle East", paper presented at Fourth Annual Conference, Centre for the Study of Islam and Democracy, Washington DC, May 16, 2003;downloaded from www.islam.democracy.org

22. Hawthorne, Amy: "Imperial Dreams: Can the Middle East Be Transformed?," Thirty-fourth in the Capitol Hill Conference Series on US Middle East Policy, Middle East Policy Council, Washington DC, October 3, 2003; downloaded from: www.mepc.org, p.8; henceforth: *Capitol Hill Conference*.

23. Etzioni, Amitai : "Democratic Coercion Could Lead

to Anarchy of Religious Societies", *Gulf News*, April 3, 2004.

24. *ibid.*

25. Bakr, Adam : "Avoid Extremism and Fear Allah", *Okaz*, Jeddah; translation printed in *Saudi Gazette*, April 4, 2004.

26. Al-Rashi, Abdul Rahman : "Time to Rescue Islam from Islamists", *Arab News*, Jeddah, June 5, 2004.

27. Al-Shayyal, Abdurrahman : "Slaughtering Our Honour", *Arab News*, Jeddah, June 20, 2004.

28. Bashir, Abdul Wahab : "Reforms to Suit Saudi Needs", *Arab News*, June 21, 2004.

29. Fuller, Graham E.: "Islamists in the Arab World: The Dance around Democracy," *Carnegie Papers*, Middle East Series, No.49, September 2004, p.13; henceforth *Fuller*.

VII. Overview and Prognosis

1. 'President Sworn-in to Second Term", Inauguration 2005; downloaded from: www.whitehouse.gov.

2. "State of the Union Address", February 2, 2005; downloaded from: www.whitehouse.gov.

3. Morales, Victor: "Democracy on the March in the Middle East?", *VOA News*, March 17, 2005; downloaded from: www.voanews.com .

4. "Democracy Stirs in the Middle East", Leader, *The Economist*, London, p.9, March 5, 2005.

5. Swain, Jon and Baxter, Sarah: "The Arabian Spring", *The Sunday Times*, London, March 6, 2005.

6. "A New Saudi Reform Memo", *Al-Quds Al-Arabi*; translation printed in *Mideast Mirror*, October 1, 2003.

7. "Saudi Reform" : text of the final communiqué and rcommendations of the second National Dialogue Forum, Makkah; translation printed in *MEES*, January 12, 2004

8. "Saudi Arabia's Rights Bodies", *Gulf News*, Dubai, March 5, 2004.

9. "Reports of High Drama at National Dialogue Exaggerated", *Arab News*, Jeddah, June 16, 2004.

10. Keynote Speech of HE Dr. Abdelouahed Belkeziz, Secretary General of the OIC, at the International Symposium on "Englightened Moderation," Islamabad, Pakistan, June 1-2, 2004.

11. Speech of HE Dr. Abdelouahed Belkeziz, Secretary General of the OIC, at the 31st ICFM, Istanbul, June 14-16, 2004; downloaded from: www.oic-oci.org ;

12. Ottaway, Marina and others: "Democratic Mirage in the Middle East", *Policy Brief*, Carnegie Endowment for International Peace, October 2002.

13. *The Economist, op.cit.*

Bibliography

A : Documents

1. Greater Middle East Partnership Initiative : published in *Middle East Economic Survey* (MEES), Nicosia, February 23, 2004.

2. The Tunis Declaration, May 23, 2004 : downloaded from www.tunisiaonline.com

3. "Broader Middle East/North Africa Partnership" and "G-8 Plan of Support for Reforms", June 9, 2004 : downloaded from www.whitehouse.gov

4. *Arab Human Development Report*-2002 : *Creating Opportunities for Future Generations* : UNDP and Arab Fund for Economic and Social Development, New York, July 2002; downloaded from : www.undp.org/rbas

5. *Arab Human Development Report*-2003 : *Building a Knowledge Society* : UNDP and Arab Fund for Economic and Social Development, New York, October 2003; downloaded from : www.undp.org/rbas

6. Saudi-US Relations : Speech Delivered by Saudi Foreign Minister Saud Al-Faisal to the Council of Foreign Relations, New York, April 27, 2004, *MEES*, Nicosia, May 3, 2004.

7. Keynote Speech of HE Dr. Abdelouahed Beleziz,

Secretary General of the OIC, to the International Symposium on "Enlightened Moderation", Islamabad, Pakistan, June 1-2, 2004; downloaded from : www.oic-oci.org

8. Speech of HE Dr. Abdelouahed Belkeziz, Secretary General of the OIC, before the 31st Session of the Islamic Conference of Foreign Ministers (ICFM), Istanbul, Turkey, June 14-16, 2004; downloaded from : www.oic-oic.org

9. Speech of HH Sheikh Hamad bin Khalifa Al Thani, Emir of Qatar, at the Opening Session of the "Democracy and Reform in the Arab World" Conference, Doha, June 3, 2004; circulated by Embassy of Qatar, Muscat, vide note 5/3/1-663, dated June 5, 2004.

B : Papers and Articles

1. Achcar, Gilbert : "Greater Middle East : The US Plan", *Le Monde diplomatique,* Paris, April 2004; translated by Paul Jones; downloaded from : www.mondediplo.com

2. Benard, Cheryl : "Civil Democratic Islam-Partners, Resources, and Strategies", National Security Research Division, *RAND Corporation,* Santa Monica, CA, 2003.

3. Carothers, Thomas and Lacina, Bethang : "Quick Transformation to Democratic Middle East is Fantasy", *Seattle Post-Intelligencer,* March 16, 2003; downloaded from : www.ceip.org

4. Fuller, Graham: "Islamists in the Arab World: The Dance around Democracy," *Carnegie Papers*, Middle East Series, No.49, September 2004.

5. Gordon, Philip H. : "Bush's Middle East Vision", *Survival*, Oxford University Press, Vol. 45, No. 1, Spring 2003, p. 155-165.

6. Hawthorne, Amy : "Can the United States Promote Democracy in the Middle East?", *Current History*, January 2003.

7. Hawthorne, Amy: "Political Reform in the Arab World: A New Ferment," *Carnegie Papers*, Middle East Series, No.52, October 2004.

8. Higgins, Andrew : "In Quest of Energy Security, US Makes New Bet: on Democracy", *Wall Street Journal*, February 4, 2004.

9. Hurd, Elizabeth Shakman : "Secularism and Democracy in the Middle East", Paper presented at Centre for the Study of Islam and Democracy, Fourth Annual Conference, Washington DC, May 16, 2003; downloaded from : www.islam-democracy.org

10. "The Broader Middle East and North Africa Initiative : Imperilled at Birth", *Middle East and North Africa Briefing*, International Crisis Group, Brussels/Amman, June 7, 2004.

11. McFaul, Michael: "Democracy Promotion as a World Value," *The Washington Quarterly*, Winter 2004-05, pp.147-63.

12. Ottaway, Marina; Carothers, Thomas; Hawthorne Amy; and Brumberg, Daniel : "Democratic Mirage in the Middle East", *Policy Brief*, Carnegie Endowment for International Peace, October 2002.

13. Ottaway, Marina : "Promoting Democracy in the Middle East – The Problem of US Credibility", Democracy and Rule of Law Project, No. 35, Carnegie Endowment for International Peace, March 2000.

14. Pollack, Kenneth, and other speakers: "Imperial Dreams: Can the Middle East Be Transformed?" Thirty-fourth in the Capitol Hill Conference Series on US Middle East Policy, Middle East Policy Council, Washington D.C., October 3, 2003; downloaded from: www.mepc.org

15. Sikand, Yoginder : "Civic, Democratic Islam", *www.outlookindia.com*, June 4, 2004.

16. Wittes, Tamara Cofman : "The New US Proposal for a Greater Middle Initiative : An Evaluation", The Brookings Institution, *Middle East Memo* #2, May 10, 2004; downloaded from : www.apps49.brookings.edu

17. Wittes, Tamara Cofman : "The Promise of Arab Liberalism", The Brookings Institution, *Policy Review*, July 2004; downloaded from : www.apps49.brookings.edu

18. Wittes, Tamara Cofman, and Yerkes, Sarah E.: "The Middle East Partnership Initiative: Progress,

Problems and Prospects," *Saban Centre Middle East Memo* #5, November 29, 2004.

19. Zakaria, Fareed : "How to Save the Arab World", *Newsweek*, December 24, 2001; downloaded from : www.msnbc.com

Newspapers/Magazines/News Services

Various issues of:

Arab News, Jeddah

Daily Star, Beirut

The Economist, London

Gulf News, Dubai

Khaleej Times, Dubai

Middle East Economic Survey, Nicosia

Mideast Mirror, London

New York Times, New York

Saudi Gazette, Jeddah

The Sunday Times, London

Times of Oman, Muscat

Washington Post, Washington DC